AUSTRALIAN
WILDFLOWER FAIRIES

This edition published 2018
By Living Book Press

1st edition published by Consolidated Press Ltd. Sydney 1937
Revised edition published 1945

ISBN: 978-0-6481048-4-1 (softcover)
         978-1-9226345-9-7 (hardcover)

NATIONAL
LIBRARY
OF AUSTRALIA

A catalogue record for this
book is available from the
National Library of Australia

AUSTRALIAN WILDFLOWER FAIRIES

by

NURI MASS

BOTANICAL
ILLUSTRATIONS

by

NURI MASS

FAIRY
ILLUSTRATIONS

by

CELESTE MASS

ALSO BY NURI MASS

Virginia Woolf, The Novelist (M.A. Thesis, Sydney Univ. 1942)
Magazine Features, published under Tina Banks nom-de-plume;
- Magic Circle
- Babe in the Woods
- Such Little Things
- The Visit
- Neighbour-Wise
- The Uninvited
- Article - Virginia Woolf
- Review - Tomorrow is Theirs
- It Couldn't Fail
- Spotlight Getaway
- Russian Mystery
- His Happiness
- The Parcel
- Foxy and I
- Fallen Leaf
- The Reason Why
- There Was, Once Upon a Time...

The Little Grammar People
The Wizard of Jenolan
Magic Australia
The Silver Candlestick
Where the Incas Trod
Randy Blair
The Wonderland of Nature
Many Paths - One Heaven
China the Waking Giant
Australian Wildflower Magic
Flowers of the Australian Alps
The Gift
Donna Roon
As Much Right To Live
Don't Kill It - It's Me
Just Give Us Time

BY CELESTE MASS

Little Miss Snipit

BY NURI MASS AND CELESTE MASS

The Australian Children's World (magazine)

*Very lovingly do I dedicate this book to my darling
MOTHER,
and also to all young Nature-lovers.*

PREFACE

Although increased interest in our native flora has recently been developed in our primary schools, much remains to be done in training the young minds to appreciate the structure and habits of our common trees, shrubs and herbs. This appreciation will never be acquired, particularly by primary school children, by mere factual instruction. It must come through an appeal to the child's emotional, imaginative and spiritual qualities—such is the purpose of this book.

The publication is unique in our Botanical and Nature Study literature, inasmuch as the numerous common trees, shrubs and herbs are invested with fairy-like qualities which will appeal to teacher and pupil alike. And how admirably adapted for such fairy lore are our little delicate Orchids, our glorious Christmas Bush, our ubiquitous Eucalypts and Wattles, our stately Waratah, and the other unique proteaceous plants! Each story has a "moral," and knowledge and appreciation of the outstanding characters of the plants will unconsciously and surely eventuate as the stories are read and appreciated. The stories are interesting and romantic, the language simple, fanciful and effective. Most of the stories are supplemented by delightfully expressed stanzas emphasising the outstanding characteristics of the plant, and for the benefit of the teacher and the pupils in the higher classes, excellent drawings and simple botanical descriptions are included. The functions of botanical structures are continually emphasised.

This publication is more than an acquisition to our Nature Study literature; it is a milestone along the path of desirable educational methods in our infant and primary schools.

E. BREAKWELL,

8/11/37   Inspector of Schools.

INTRODUCTION

My dear little Reader,—

Of course, you know that every bushland flower has a fairy all to itself. In reality, cityland flowers have fairies also, but in the city there are so many people hurrying about all day long, most of them having nothing whatsoever to do with fairies, calling them "nonsense" and other terrible names like that, that they have been frightened away; and although they do sometimes enter a mortal garden to love and protect those whose names and appearance they bear, they live nearly always high above the earth and above the clouds in a beautiful place called Fairyland.

But in the bush—in those dark, mossy, secret nooks where mortals very seldom venture, and also hidden in the grasses of the open country—throngs of tiny, shimmering fairies love to dwell, with those delicate flowers who are just as shy and timid as they; for fairies, as you know, are the souls of flowers!

Now, quite a short time ago, at that dark blue hour of twilight, I happened to be walking through a very quiet, unvisited portion of our bush, and I was thinking of many things—but principally of fairies. And the more I thought the sadder I grew, for I remembered what shy wee creatures they were, and how careful they had to be never to be seen by mortal eyes.

"Alas," said I aloud to myself, "how very unfortunate are humans—and how unhappy am **I**, being a human!"

But as sorrow always serves to make us weary, I began to feel all of a sudden as if I could walk no farther; so I sat down on a little bank of green grass, and, for no particular reason at all, picked two or three Bluebells that were growing nearby.

Now, the night was becoming darker and more magic every minute—and, of course, I must have shaken those Bluebells a good deal as I picked them. So I dare say you can imagine for yourself what happened. All the wildflower fairies, hovering about not **very** far away, had heard the tiny tinkling of bells; and almost as soon as I had picked the fairy flowers, I saw a rapid movement through the grass. Then my eye alighted on a little yellow Orchid—then I saw a green and a pink one. Beside them was a shrub covered with Mountain Devil flowers, and creeping over it a long strand of snowy Clematis. In fact, there were so many flowers all around me, that I thought the whole bush was trying to crowd on to my bank of green grass.

They looked stationary enough, but in reality they were all disturbed! I knew it, and I told them so. Upon hearing that I loved them and did not want to hurt them, but to be made their immediate friend, they gradually began to peep out with shiny little fairy eyes—yes! they **were** fairies! And one by one, they told me their sweet stories, and sang me the prettiest songs.

And it was because I felt sure that you also would love to hear them that I have written them down for you, just the way I heard them myself.

I do hope you are going to enjoy them as I did.

—NURI MASS.

A NOTE FROM THE AUTHOR'S CHILDREN

We have updated this edition, coming about 80 years after our 18-year old mother wrote the original version, to give more detail in some areas. We have:

- appended her flower diagram from "The Wonderland of Nature" to show the names of flower parts, shown in the Contents under "Diagram of a Flower";
- changed the sex of the 'worker bees' that visit flowers to female, since male 'drone' bees generally stay in their hives until their mating flight;
- updated some flower names; and
- described in more detail how plants make sugars, and what a 'kino' is.

At the time this book was first published and became a recommended school textbook, its imaginative images and storylines fitted in well with those of contemporaneous Australian author-artists such as May Gibbs and Ida Rentoul Outhwaite. We do hope that now, retaining this old-world reverence for the magic in our unique Australian bushland, this book can find a new enchanted audience and help us to better understand and cherish our natural world.

Tess and Chris Horwitz

2018

CONTENTS

FAIRY

ILLUSTRATIONS

"What very pleasant weather!"

The Knight of the Fairy Garter

(CRYPTOSTYLIS—type subulata)

Red and yellow and green and brown,
My name, Cryptostylis subulata;
Bold and daring I stand erect:
I am the Knight of the Fairy Garter!

Yes, indeed, I am a very noble Orchid, and I am always accomplishing such chivalrous deeds that all my Orchid relations seem to look up to me a great deal.

Do you see the large dark green leaf (as people call it) which I wear at the bottom of my plant? Well, in reality, that is my shield, and it is a great protection for me, as you can well imagine. Unlike most of my relations, I only have one very significant petal. It is called my "labellum"; and as I am so proud of my honourable title, I wear my garter in the form of three little black stripes from one end of it nearly to the other.

And talking about relations, I can tell you a secret about them. I think they are rather sensitive of it, for none of them ever mention a word of it— but nearly all of them stand up-side-down, that is to say, on their heads. Personally, I think it a little undignified, and that is another reason why I am so different and why I gain such respect; I stand on my feet! For my part, I have never heard of a noble achieving such distinction as Knight of the Garter on his head, have you?

I suppose it is partly because I realise the great majesty of my position that I do not bother to arrive in perfect time, and mostly make my appearance a little late. A quarter-past Summer is far more becoming, I think, than five minutes to spring.

I am an enthusiastic listener of every passing breeze's symphony and the glory of the bush-birds' choir; also a keen spectator of every butterfly's toe-dancing exhibition. If you wish to meet me in Nature's theatre, you will usually find me with several of my own family in the dress-circle, sitting in grassy seats on the very tops of hills.

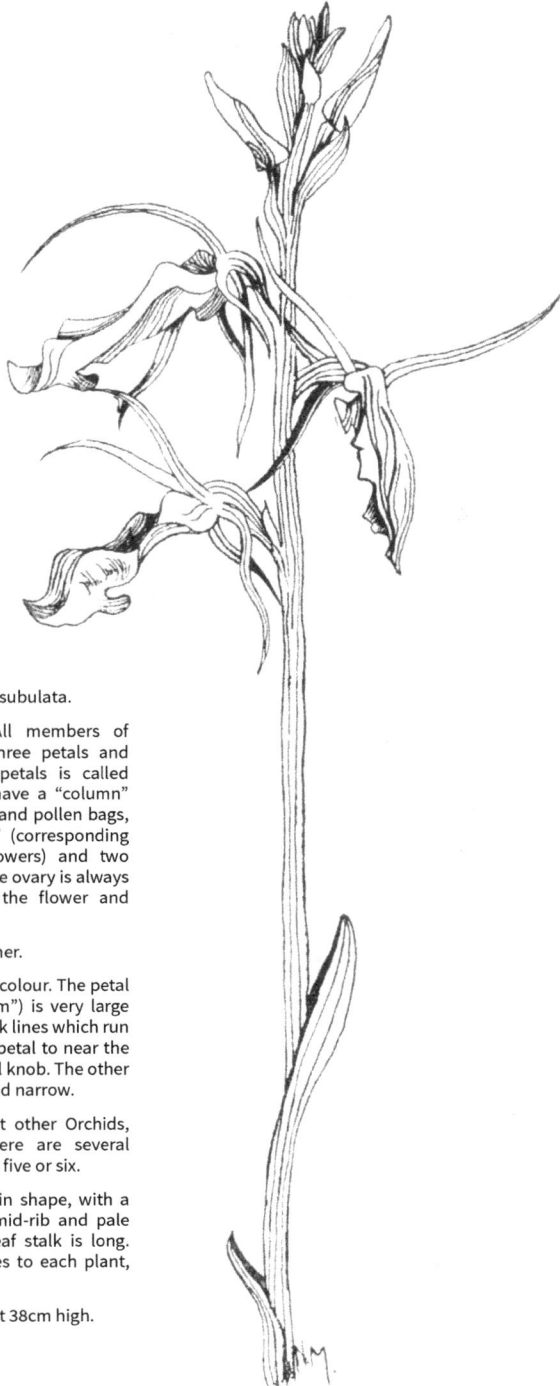

CRYPTOSTYLIS—type subulata.

Family: Orchidaceae. All members of family Orchidaceae have three petals and three sepals, One of the petals is called the "labellum". Also, they have a "column" which consists of an anther and pollen bags, a "sticky stigmatic surface" (corresponding to the stigma in other flowers) and two "appendages" or "wings." The ovary is always below the other parts of the flower and consists of three carpels.

Flowering season: summer.

Flowers: Dark reddish in colour. The petal called the "lip" (or "labellum") is very large and has three prominent dark lines which run from near the base of each petal to near the tip, where they end in a small knob. The other petals and sepals are long and narrow.

The flowers, unlike most other Orchids, are not up-side-down. There are several flowers on the stem—usually five or six.

Leaves: Long, and oval in shape, with a glossy surface, prominent mid-rib and pale green under-surface. The leaf stalk is long. There are about three leaves to each plant, or less.

Usually, the plant is about 38cm high.

The Mountain Devil
(LAMBERTIA—type formosa)

Do you know what it is like to be trapped in a huge jungle, where everything is tangled together and trying to tangle round you too?

Well, if you could be like Alice in Wonderland, and have some of the things happening to you that once happened to her, you would perhaps eat a little piece of mushroom which would make you grow smaller and smaller, until you were only the size of an ant.

Maybe you would think that exciting. But there are always faults to be found, even in the choicest of adventures. And so, being the size of a little brown ant, you would most likely feel inclined to get into all the mischief that an ant gets into. And one of the very first things you would do would be to sniff round a little and say to yourself:

"Honey! I smell honey! And I am very fond of honey!" Then, you would set out to find it, only to discover that it was lying hidden away, deep down in my flower.

You would be rather careless after this and, not taking as a hint the fact that I had concealed it so carefully, you would begin your dangerous descent down my little tunnel of flame-coloured petals. And what would you meet there? Why! You would find yourself in a dark, dense jungle of—oh, all sorts of creepy, frightening things. They would only be a number of soft, fluffy hairs in reality. But you, being so small, would think otherwise, and would realise for the first time that you were not wanted.

Of course, you would try ever so hard to escape then. You would stumble over one hair, and fall on your head over another, and turn a double somersault over the next.

But in the end, you would manage to get out, and, feeling yourself once more in the open air, you would look back at me and threaten me a good deal, and say that without any doubt I was a huge, or an immense, or a "mountainous" devil!

I wonder if that is truly why I am called the "Mountain Devil," or whether my name also comes from the fact that my home is often on the hills and mountain-tops?

Of course, although I admit that I am somewhat of a devil in my own way, I must make you feel certain, little reader, that I am not of the really

14

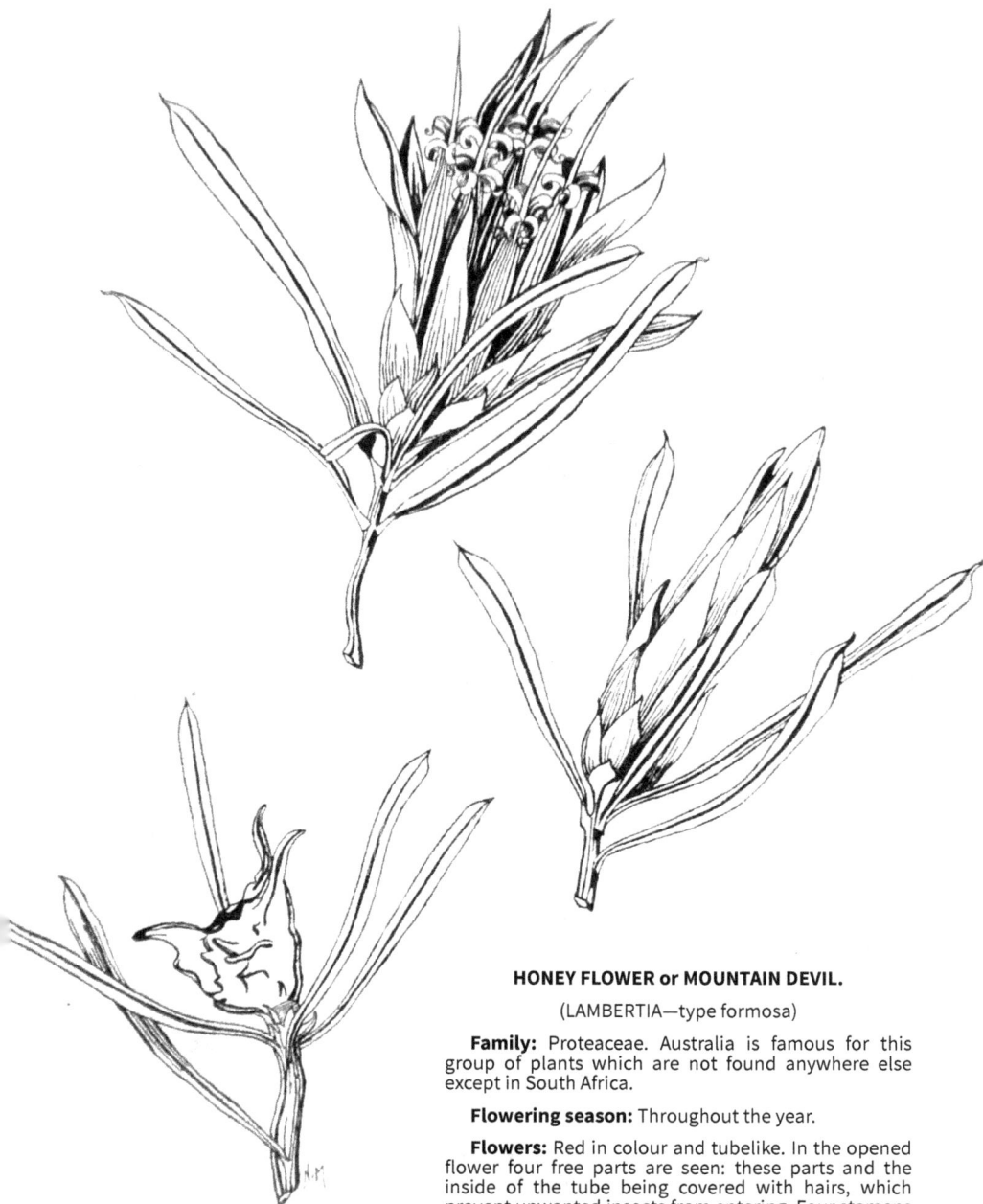

HONEY FLOWER or MOUNTAIN DEVIL.

(LAMBERTIA—type formosa)

Family: Proteaceae. Australia is famous for this group of plants which are not found anywhere else except in South Africa.

Flowering season: Throughout the year.

Flowers: Red in colour and tubelike. In the opened flower four free parts are seen: these parts and the inside of the tube being covered with hairs, which prevent unwanted insects from entering. Four stamens are placed on the petals. In the flower the pistil stands out far beyond the petal parts. There are usually six or seven blooms in a group at the end of the stem, surrounded by little satiny leaves, called "bracts", which entirely cover the buds. Honeysuckers usually carry the pollen from flower to flower, and they can therefore be called "pollinators".

Fruit: A woody box, whose peculiar shape gave the name of "Mountain Devil." This box contains two seeds which have wings.

villainous type; for a flower or a fairy could never be cruel. I am fond of mischief, that's all. My whole existence is mischief, you know—even to the beautiful colours of my flowers, and the satiny leaves that protect them when they are still buds. Because, just when human visitors to bushland are thinking how sweet and harmless I appear, I begin to drop my satiny leaves (which botanists call "bracts") and also my flame-coloured petals, leaving only a funny, fantastic-looking little head, which is green at first, but which gets hard and brown as it grows larger.

It has a long, pointed nose, and two long, pointed horns. (You can see its portrait on the previous page).

Naturally, when they pass me again a few days afterwards and see what has happened, they are absolutely bewildered, and they whisper stories about my being a devil in disguise.

Then, when they come up to look at me more closely, I cannot resist the temptation to prick their fingers or noses with the sharp, needle-like ends of my foliage leaves.

Oh, you should see how they jump when this happens—and get away as quickly as possible, without even looking back to see how my whole bush is simply shaking with laughter.

Some flowers, I know, like to make their appearance only in one or two seasons of the year. For me, that would seem a most unexciting form of existence—especially as my flowers are my chief helpers in mischief-making.

And that is why you will probably see several bright splashes of red and orange colour on my bushes whenever you happen to pass me—regardless of time or weather.

> Be careful, be careful, little human child!
> The woods are weird and haunted,
> The woods are strange and wild.
> A tiny Mountain Devil may spring upon your path,
> And with his fiery eye
> May ask the reason why
> You've chanced within his secret haunts.
> And if your answer is not good,
> Or if he has not understood,
> He'll quickly grab you by the hair
> And drag you to a goblin's lair!
> And after this you'll never go
> Too near where Mountain Devils grow!

"Became a little azure flower."

The Twilight Fairy

(THELYMITRA——type grandiflora)

Although humans mostly call me the Great Sun Orchid, amongst the fairy-folk I am always known as the Orchid of Twilight; for indeed, my blooms, which are large and numerous, are very much like the sky at twilight—that deep velvety blue, almost purple colour, still tinged with the golden kiss of a lingering sunbeam.

And do you know how this came about in the very beginning? Well, then, I shall tell you:

> One evening when the sky was blue,
> And tinted with a rosy hue,
> A host of tiny fairy things
> On starry dust-besprinkled wings
> Flew up above the clouds of snow,
> Beyond our mortal sight, and lo!
> There fell upon the earth well nigh
> Ten million pieces of the sky—
> Which each, through mystic fairy power,
> Became a little azure flower.
> Alas! The elves complaining came;
> "The sky will never be the same,
> With all the holes that you have left
> Through sheer destruction-love and theft!"
> The fairies laughed in happy glee:
> "Oh, silly ones, you soon will see;
> For fairies could not beauty mar"—
> Each space became a twinkling star!

GREAT SUN ORCHID

(THELYMITRA—type grandiflora)

Family: Orchidaceae.

Flowering season: Spring and early summer.

Flowers: Vary from almost purple colour to light blue. They are large and numerous. The centre (or column) is comparatively large and very elegant.

Leaves: Long and broad.

The Lament of the Sundew Fairy

(DROSERA—type binata)

In the kingdom of flowers and fairies, I am sorry to say that I belong to Cannibal Island. Perhaps little human boys may think that a most exciting home, filled to the brim with adventures. But, strange as it may seem, I am a sad and lonely wildflower—because, you see, I am the cannibal.

Now, if you listen to my story I think you will understand how it is that I do such cruel things, and that I am left so very much alone by all the fairy-folk.

Doubtless you have often heard your human friends mention the name Sundew. Well, that means me—or else one of my near relations. The name is really a good one, I think, because when the sun shines down on me, my long, forked leaves look just as if they were covered with crystal dewdrops. As you can imagine, they are very pretty indeed. All humans think they are, and so do flies, ants and other tiny insects.

But here is where the tragic part begins. Those little sparkling things are not dewdrops at all. They are the sticky ends of simply dozens of long, fine hairs.

Now, when Sir Fly or WilliamAnt, Esq. comes along to admire them, they immediately chuckle to themselves and with a loud shout (which mortals never heat, but which I always do hear) of "Ha! Trapped!" they close down all over their poor wee victim, holding him tightly, as if with a hundred strong arms. Of course, he cannot possibly breathe, and so in a very few minutes he dies, and my plant eats him up.

Oh, the heart of my flower sinks with sorrow when this happens, but it can never do anything to save the lives of inquisitive insects who will go inspecting my attractive leaves.

Often and often I hold up my five petals (which have grown so pale with worry that they are now milky white) and warn passing small beetles, flies, mosquitoes, and so on:

"Oh, please, do not go near my leaves, little friends. You will go to your death! You will go to your death!"

But they look back at me over their shoulders, and call out their answer to me:

"Silly, timid flower! We're not afraid of anything—just watch us. We're not afraid!"

And with this, of course, they daringly alight upon those cruel, deceiving "dewdrops." And in the next morning's "Bushland News" there appears a startling account of the heart-rending deaths of Mademoiselle Mosquito and Senor Beetle at the hands of cannibal Sundew.

No wonder elves and fairies shun my company. No wonder I am the loneliest and saddest of all wildflowers!

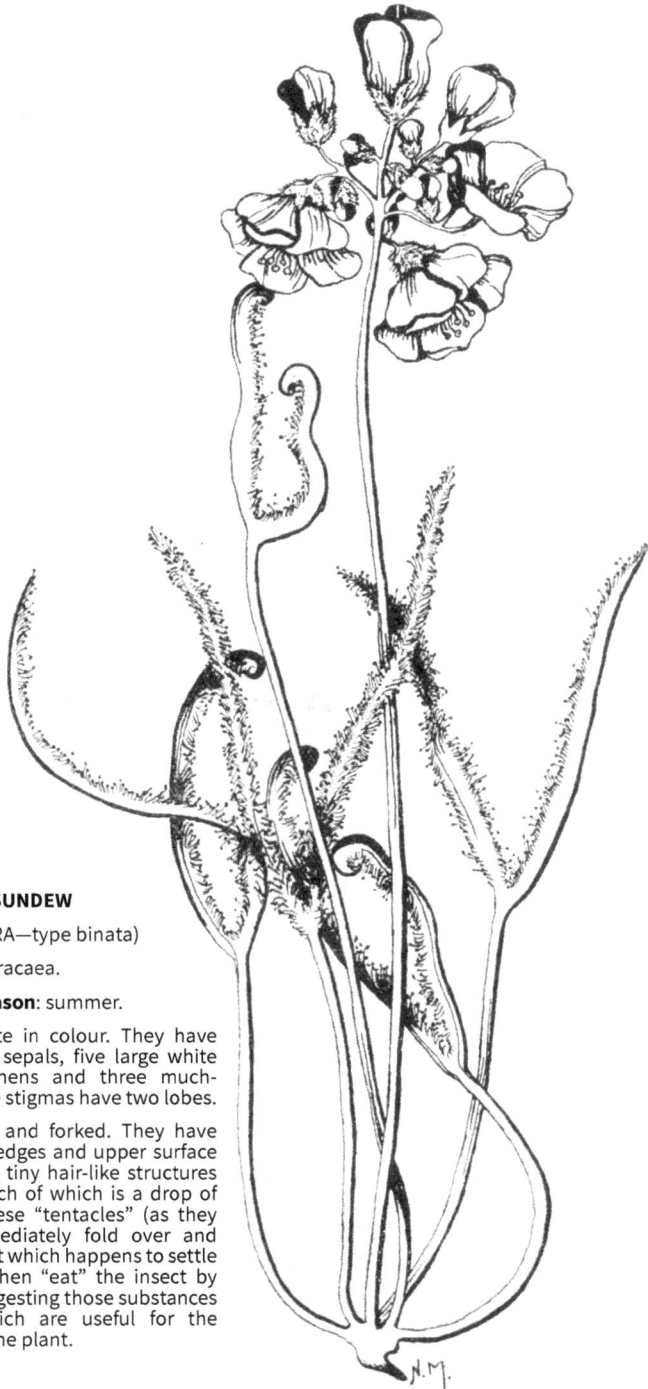

SUNDEW

(DROSERA—type binata)

Family: Droseracaea.

Flowering season: summer.

Flowers: White in colour. They have five small green sepals, five large white petals, five stamens and three much-forked styles. The stigmas have two lobes.

Leaves: Long and forked. They have long stalks. The edges and upper surface are covered with tiny hair-like structures on the top of each of which is a drop of sticky liquid. These "tentacles" (as they are called) immediately fold over and around any insect which happens to settle on them. They then "eat" the insect by dissolving and digesting those substances of its body which are useful for the nourishment of the plant.

The Boronia Fairy

(BORONIA—type ledifolia)

Sometimes I cannot help wishing that I was only a common little weed, prized by fairies and despised by humans; for, in that case, my life would be much happier than it is.

Somebody called "the Government" (about whom I know very little indeed) has declared me "protected," and has forbidden people from picking me without special permission. But I am afraid my life is almost as perilous as it would be if I were not protected at all, because people just do not seem to take much notice of what the Government says.

Quite often, of course, poor humans come along and gather great armfuls of me to sell in the city streets to rich humans. I do not resent this in the slightest (as long as they pick me when I am growing in gardens) for although sometimes the smoke and dust of busy streets nearly choke me, I know that I am helping to buy food and clothing for those who are really in need. And my heart simply bounds for joy when I am carried into a room where someone is lying ill, because, although again I find it difficult not to choke with all the queer unpleasant odours filling the air, I know that I am bringing happiness to one who may be sad.

But when cruel, thoughtless mortals come tramping down the bush-tracks, doing nothing except destroying everywhere they go, my whole plant quivers with fear, and my bright pink flowers try in vain to hide amongst the bushes surrounding them. Mostly I have great cause for fear, because the next moment I find myself being whisked along the track—high up in the air or dragged along the ground—far, far away from my happy home. And I have not been picked with any regard to my feelings either, but pulled up by my very roots—which is a most terrible and lamentable thing. You would think so too if it happened to you.

So you can see what a dangerous and uncertain existence a prized bush-flower has to live, and why I began by telling you that at times I wished I was only a common little weed, can't you?

Now although we Boronias are Australian plants some of the other members of our family are very fond of life on the Continent. These are what people call the citrus fruits—like oranges, lemons and mandarins. You may be surprised to hear that I have a lemon for my cousin, because we look so very different from one another. But if you examine us again closely,

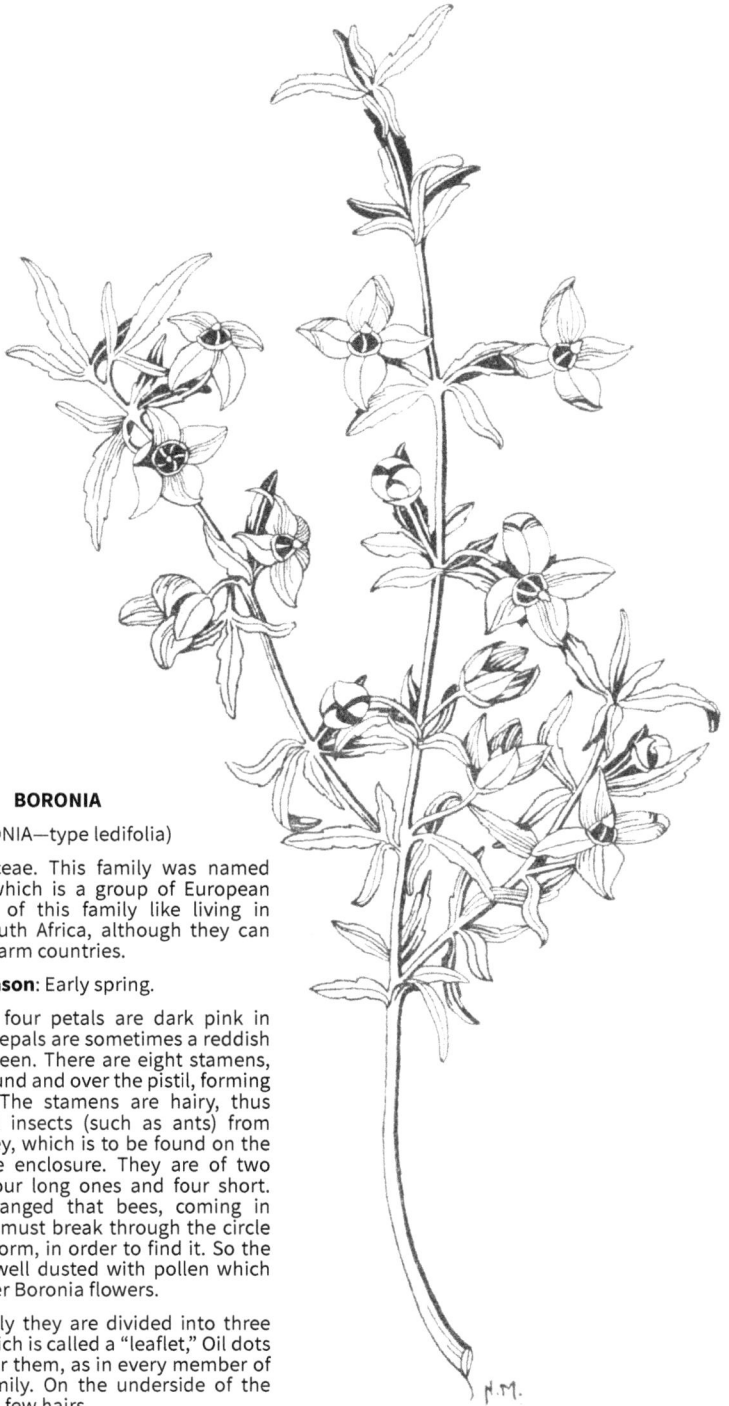

BORONIA

(BORONIA—type ledifolia)

Family: Rutaceae. This family was named after the Ruta, which is a group of European herbs. Members of this family like living in Australia and South Africa, although they can grow well in all warm countries.

Flowering season: Early spring.

Flowers: The four petals are dark pink in colour. The four sepals are sometimes a reddish colour or dark green. There are eight stamens, which close in round and over the pistil, forming a sort of cage. The stamens are hairy, thus preventing small insects (such as ants) from stealing the honey, which is to be found on the floor of the little enclosure. They are of two different sizes: four long ones and four short. They are so arranged that bees, coming in search of honey, must break through the circle which their tips form, in order to find it. So the insects become well dusted with pollen which they carry to other Boronia flowers.

Leaves: Usually they are divided into three parts, each of which is called a "leaflet." Oil dots are visible all over them, as in every member of the Rutaceae family. On the underside of the leaves there are a few hairs.

23

you will see that we really are alike in many things. The formation of our flowers is similar, in spite of the fact that orange- and lemon-blossoms have five petals and sepals whilst I have only four, and also different numbers of stamens from mine.

And there is something else by which you can always recognise a member of my family (Rutaceae by name) when you see it. If you hold the leaves of a Rutaceae plant up to the light, you will notice all over them tiny round specks of a whitish colour. These are, in reality, little glands filled with oil. This oil gives the plant a strange scent which, because it is disliked by animals that live on herbs, helps to protect the plant against them and the damage they might cause.

Have you ever noticed the funny little cage that my stamens form around my pistil? If not, you should look for it next time you come across me, as it is worth seeing. Each wee stamen is a separate bar. In this way, the pistil is well protected from the heat and brightness of day.

Now, on the floor of the cage is the honey; and when Ms. Bee comes along to take her share of it, she must push her head down through the circle formed by my anthers, in order to find it. So that when, after quite a little while, she drags her head out again, she looks as funny as anything—just as if she were wearing a yellow powdered wig. We flowers laugh at her ever so much; but, owing to the honey she has quaffed, she is feeling in merry mood, and gaily buzzes off to another pink bloom without the slightest offence.

"Ungrateful he, who pluck'd thee from thy stalk,
Poor faded flow'ret! On his careless way;
Inhal'd awhile thy odours on his walk,
Then onward pass'd and left thee to decay.

Ah! melancholy emblem! had I seen
Thy modest beauties dew'd with Evening's gem,
I had not rudely cropp'd thy parent stem,
But left thee, blushing, 'mid the enliven'd green."

—Coleridge.

The Song of the Blackberry Fairy

(RUBUS—type fruticosus)

A restless and mischievous wildflower am I,
As white as the clouds in the clear azure sky.
My home is now here, my home is now there—
My home, to speak truly, is 'most everywhere.
An elegant bramble I never could be:
Politest society shudders at me,
For ne'er was there anyone under the sun
Enamoured, as I am, of mischief and fun!

A delicate morsel, for instance, are socks,
And pieces of petticoats, jackets and frocks.
As children are passing, upon them I seize—
And mostly they leave me a bit of their knees.
But frightful discomfiture everyone knows
If e'er I should catch at the tip of his nose.
For pleasure untold is a little hooked thorn,
Yet mortals think only of things that it's torn.

But I am forgiven—and even by **them**
When black, luscious berries appear on each stem!

BLACKBERRY

(RUBUS—type fructicosus)

Family: Rosaceae. This is the family to which the Rose and many fruit blossoms belong.

Flowering season: Spring (usually).

Flowers: They have five green hairy sepals, five large white petals, many stamens and pistils.

Leaves: Usually large, and divided into three leaflets (although the number of leaflets varies). There are small thorns on the under-surface along the mid-rib.

The stalks of the leaves as well as the main stalks have large thorns.

Fruit: Green when young; dark purple when ripe. They are arranged in clusters. When ripe they are very juicy. Each fruit is one-seeded.

The Wild Parsley Fairy

(LOMATIA—type silaifolia)

You take it quite for granted that birds, bees, moths and butterflies have wings, do you not? And yet, I wonder if you have ever thought of flowers as having them, too? Indeed, so usual is it to consider the plant world as stationary, that even flowers themselves forget sometimes, and bemoan their adventure-less existences.

But now, when you start to think about it a little, you will realise that there are some plants which are to be found not only in one country but throughout many others as well. How, then, can anyone imagine that their whole lives are spent in the one spot and in the one little piece of soil?

"Oh," I can hear you answering me, "That is easy to explain. The plant grows and dies exactly where it has been sown. Then, next year, seeds grow into other plants, which in their turn live exactly where they have been sown."

But you must be careful not to think of these little seeds as being something quite apart from the plant which you are able to see, holding its leaves and branches up in the golden sunlight, and thrusting its roots into the dark soil. For, since they are formed actually inside the flowers of those plants, they must be just as much a part of them as are the flowers themselves.

And now, if we should follow the journeyings of ripe wee seeds which have broken away from their long imprisonment, we would surely never think again that a plant's whole life is one of inactivity.

Some seeds, when they gain their freedom, like to fly—others to float, others to swim, and others are so lazy that they depend on being carried away by passing animals, to whose furry coats they cling as tightly as they can with tiny needle-like structures and spikes.

But since, of all these and many other ways, my seeds always prefer to fly, I am naturally more interested in that form of travelling than in any of the rest.

Flying, of course, needs wings or (in my case as well as in numerous others) only one wing, so that, attached to the end of each of my seeds, you will see a long, brown, papery structure which answers my purpose well, and by means of which my seed is able to travel extensively and see quite a lot of the bush before it settles down and decides to grow.

Do you not think it rather pretty, little reader, that a very part of the flower which has spent so long a time in one unchanging place should at last go free into the world-—a tiny being filled with sleeping life—ready to burst forth at the given moment into a new and beautiful plant the same as that from which it itself has come?

WILD PARSLEY

(LOMATIA—type silaifolia)

Family: Proteaceae.

Flowering season: Summer, but sometimes even winter.

Flowers: Cream coloured, with four petals, four stamens joined to the petals and a curved style. Before the petals fall off they become separated from one another. The flowers are arranged in pairs up the stem.

Leaves: Much divided and of firm texture.

Seeds: Winged. The fruit is a black-coloured box. Between the seeds, a yellow-coloured dust can be seen.

The Story of the Tall Greenhood Fairy

(PTEROSTYLIS—type longifolia)

Just the same as humans have proper as well as nicknames, we flowers have them too; and so it is that although I am formally called Pterostylis, I am affectionately called Greenhood. I must admit that Greenhood sounds prettier and more homely; but all the same, I wish I could hear my other name too, more often, because then, you see I would know that mortals were taking a keener interest in me.

That large bonnet which I always wear, and those long, fine feelers are rather pretty, don't you think? I simply love you to take notice of them, for naturally, flowers long to be loved by everyone. But I feel very particularly happy if the musical mosquitoes admire them, for I can never be quite sure of humans, but mosquitoes are always kind to me. Of course, they have no idea they are being kind; but please do not tell them I said so, because they may get awfully offended and not come near me any more. One learns from experience that mosquitoes are funny things to deal with, and inclined to become somewhat peeved if flowers do not appreciate them thoroughly.

As well as my prettily coloured flowers, I also keep something else which I am sure will tempt them to visit me. It is a sort of sweet-tasting liquid—and if you have ever entered into an intimate conversation with a mosquito, you will already know how fond he is of being entertained with a little something to eat and drink.

Well, the smallest one of my petals is what many people call my "tongue," and this petal is very, very sensitive; so that when the tiny visitor comes along and steps upon it even as gently as can be, it suddenly springs up from its hanging-down position, thus holding him entrapped—but not quite! There is still a tiny open passage through which he can escape; and I have taken the greatest care that in retreating by this one and only outlet, he must brush past my ripe pollen bags, which quickly shake off some of their fine yellow dust right over that funny little hump on his back.

Now he flies away, singing and buzzing in sheer joy at having regained his freedom. And then, so that he may enjoy his adventure again, he makes his way to another Orchid the same as I, and walks straight in. But, as he does so, he passes by the very sticky stigma where, of course, some of the pollen gets caught—and only then has it reached its destination.

As you can see, this saves me a great deal of trouble, for no flowers can

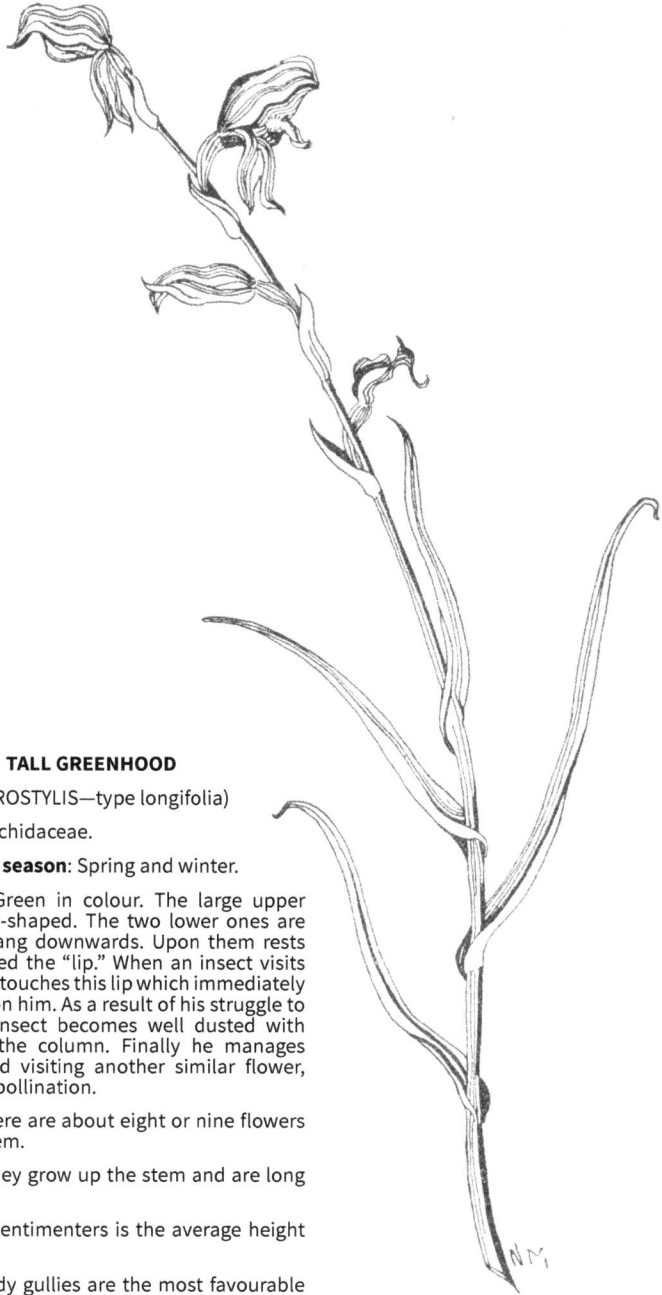

TALL GREENHOOD

(PTEROSTYLIS—type longifolia)

Family: Orchidaceae.

Flowering season: Spring and winter.

Flowers: Green in colour. The large upper sepal is hood-shaped. The two lower ones are joined and hang downwards. Upon them rests the petal called the "lip." When an insect visits the flower, he touches this lip which immediately springs over on him. As a result of his struggle to escape, the insect becomes well dusted with pollen from the column. Finally he manages to escape and visiting another similar flower, brings about pollination.

Usually there are about eight or nine flowers on the one stem.

Leaves: They grow up the stem and are long and pointed.

About 30 centimenters is the average height of the plant.

Moist, shady gullies are the most favourable positions for its growth.

grow into more flowers unless their pollen is carried from one to the other. If Mr. Mosquito did not oblige me, just think of the terrible amount of walking about I would have to do!

And now, little mortal child, if you have grown to love me as I love you, please come and visit me whenever you can. My address is:

Amongst mosses and maiden-hair,

Fern-strewn gullies.

And the date of my appearance is winter and spring.

Mosquitoes like to be entertained.

The Wattle Fairy

(ACACIA—type longifolia, variety typica)

Often I think that the members of family Wattle (which are very numerous indeed—far more so than those of any human family) are similar to mortals in at least one respect: in that there are short, round Wattles, long, thin ones, short, thin ones, and long, fat ones. In other words, there is every possible shape of Wattle, just the same as there is every possible shape of human. Although (I may be biased in this) I always think that Wattles possess a stronger claim to elegance than do humans.

Well, of all these kinds, I am a long and fat one, and as I am to be found quite plentifully in many places, I am sure you must have seen and picked me often. I hope that when you pass by me next time, along some bush-track, you will lean over and whisper something in my ear about my being pretty to look at. Now, you may think me vain, and perhaps you think rightly, but I have to admit that with nearly all flowers, vanity is a very common fault.

Have you ever looked at my leaves closely, little human? I wonder. If you have, you will have noticed how long and flat they are. Yet in reality—and here is the funny part of it—they are not leaves at all, but flattened stems. You see, Australia is rather a hot, dry country to live in; and the sun, although he is responsible for our continued lives, can also be very cruel, and can steal from us with his heat the water which we drink from the earth and which saves us from dying of thirst and hunger.

So that, it would be an easy thing for us just to die away and be forgotten. But, dear Mother Nature, who is so gentle and so wise, could never allow anything like that to happen. And that is why she has flattened out my stems for me, making them look like leaves. For stems are generally more careful, and are able to store valuable food that leaves would simply give over to Father Sun with very little more than a word.

I suppose you have often heard it said that the Wattle is the national flower of Australia; and in case you do not know why this should be, I shall tell you straight away. It is because, out of the five hundred members of my family, three hundred live in Australia, and only two hundred have chosen to go abroad. How would you like to have four hundred and nine-nine brothers and sisters, as I have? I can assure you it is very interesting— you see, I can claim relationship to so many of the flowers in Bushland. But remembering all their names is not quite so pleasant—especially as they are always ready to accuse me of neglect if I mix them up a bit.

WATTLE

(ACACIA—type longfolia, variety typica)

Family: Leguminosae. The special group to which the Wattles belong is called Mimosae. All members of this family have "legumes" or pods as their fruits. This is why the name "Leguminosae" has been given to the family.

Flowering season: Spring, summer, and sometimes even autumn.

Flowers: There are many minute flowers closely crowded together all over fairly long stems. Each flower has five tiny sepals and five tiny petals, together with very many stamens. The petals, sepals and stamens are all the same colour—bright yellow.

Leaves: The leaf stalks are flattened and act as the leaves. They are broad and up to 45cm long. They have clear parallel and cross veinings.

Fruit: A very narrow pod. The positions of the seeds can be seen easily by means of protuberances along the pod.

Then there are those two hundred in other parts of the world (mostly in the tropics of the Southern Hemisphere)—they are another problem. I wish they would all come over to Australia, and make correspondence a little less difficult. Sometimes years go by, and I do not hear from one of them, and not one of them hears from me.

But we are really a very happy family. In fact, our soft, pretty flowers (varying in colour from pure white to deep yellow) are so abundant and make our bushes look so bright, that, amongst humans, they seem to be actual symbols of happiness.

Oh, golden are the gumleaves as the zephyrs o'er them blow,
And golden is the sunny light that makes them shimmer so.
And Autumn colours other leaves with hues so wondrous bold
That when they fall, they spread the earth with canopies of gold!

The little wand'ring buttercup that haunts the riverside
Is brilliant gold—and in her heart the golden nectar hides.
The azure heavens golden turn when lit with sunset glow;
And golden are my stamens a-swaying to and fro!

My pollen dust is golden-hued, which in my flower I hold,
And insects, when they brush me by, are also dusted gold.
I love to see the woodlands, with all my shrubs in bloom,
Transformed to Springtide's golden life from Winter's misty gloom!

" . . . . each beauteous flower,
Iris all hues, roses, and jessamine
Reared high their flourished heads between, and wrought
Mosaic; underfoot the violet,
Crocus, and hyacinth, with rich inlay
Broidered the ground, more coloured than with stone
Of costliest emblem."

—Milton.

The Waratah Fairy

(TELOPEA—type speciosissima)

The shy Wild Violet, drooping her head over a woodland stream, says sadly to me: "Ah, you are a bold and hardened flower. You are so sure of your great beauty that there is no sweet timidity in you."

The dainty Bluebell nods to and fro as she chimes in: "Yes, you are haughty indeed, and have no time to talk with your little companions who have not grown as tall and majestic as you."

Then says the wicked Mountain Devil: "There is no mischief in your eye; there is no impishness in your ways. You are always cold and reserved, and give me a disdainful glance every time I prick or make faces at anyone. I do not, I cannot, I will not, like you!" And with this, his wrathful bush shakes so much and stamps its roots so peevishly into the earth, that all the lovely red flowers fall off, and very soon the shrub is covered with dozens of little devil-heads.

Now, you may think that all this abuse makes my life one long misery. But there you are mistaken, for it amuses me ever so much and helps to bring a little variety into my life.

But I do not only **hear** these remarks; sometimes I actually manage to bend my very stiff neck just enough to see the speakers. When they notice that I am looking at them closely, they usually feel a bit ashamed of themselves. The little Violet is very sweet and, having smiled at me, as much as to say: "Do not misunderstand me, Sir Waratah; I was really only teasing, and right inside me I am truly fond of you," and she fixes her eyes upon her image in the stream. Young Bluebell tries to pretend that nothing whatsoever had been said, and that my inspection had not been noticed, by giving voice to a long chorus of "Ding dong, ding dong, ding dong bell" without even glancing in my direction.

Also, it happens at times that when Mountain Devil, in a spasm of extra peevishness, buries four or five of his sharply-pointed leaves into my stalk, I look down suddenly at him with a frown. Of course, his guilty conscience tells him that my face is fiery red with anger; the result being that I do not hear or feel anything else from him for quite a long time—perhaps even ten minutes.

However, I am not angry, for I must admit that I have a very even temper, being mostly that "cool, calm and collected" type.

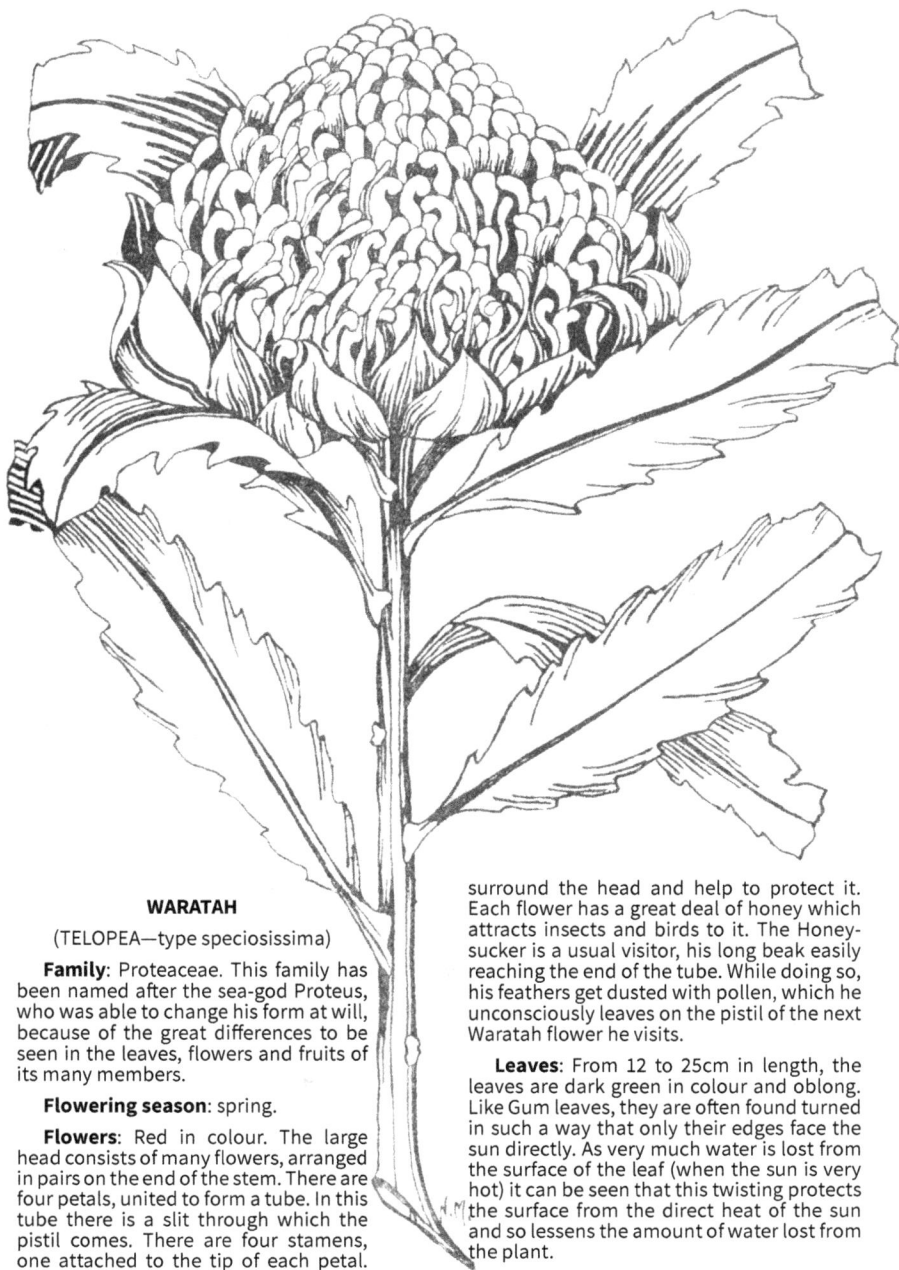

WARATAH

(TELOPEA—type speciosissima)

Family: Proteaceae. This family has been named after the sea-god Proteus, who was able to change his form at will, because of the great differences to be seen in the leaves, flowers and fruits of its many members.

Flowering season: spring.

Flowers: Red in colour. The large head consists of many flowers, arranged in pairs on the end of the stem. There are four petals, united to form a tube. In this tube there is a slit through which the pistil comes. There are four stamens, one attached to the tip of each petal. When the pollen is ripe, the tips of the petals roll back and the pistil springs to an upright position. Many large bracts surround the head and help to protect it. Each flower has a great deal of honey which attracts insects and birds to it. The Honeysucker is a usual visitor, his long beak easily reaching the end of the tube. While doing so, his feathers get dusted with pollen, which he unconsciously leaves on the pistil of the next Waratah flower he visits.

Leaves: From 12 to 25cm in length, the leaves are dark green in colour and oblong. Like Gum leaves, they are often found turned in such a way that only their edges face the sun directly. As very much water is lost from the surface of the leaf (when the sun is very hot) it can be seen that this twisting protects the surface from the direct heat of the sun and so lessens the amount of water lost from the plant.

Fruit: A long pod, which splits open on one side and sets free many seeds, each of which has a long wing attached to it.

The flowers who grow only to a small height think my existence must be wearisome and uninteresting, away up in the air. But, of course, they are quite wrong, for I have the loveliest friends imaginable. I am nearer to the Lillipilly than they are, and to the Christmas Bush and Wattle and Gum and ever so many others. These are my friends, and we have the most enlightening conversations at times about the sunshine and the storm clouds, the winds and the rains.

Then also, there is Mr. Honeysucker, who is extremely amiable, and who brings us news from all over Bushland. He is far more interesting, I am sure, than any of the newspapers which mortals leave around us sometimes. These seem concerned only with armies and navies and the making of machine guns. But Mr. Honeysucker tells us of the amazing industry of ants, which enables them to build immense homes for themselves so quickly. He relates to us the doings of the famous Blue wren family that lives in such a tree round such a bend in the bush track leading to such a place—and of Billy the Bullfinch and Christopher the Kingfisher. News of this description is, it seems to me, far more profitable than any of quarrels and wars.

You must already know me very well, little human, so there is hardly need for me to describe myself. You must not think for a moment, however, that my large crimson head is only one flower; for it is very many flowers all crowded together, the top ones of which are "slow-coaches" and are still to be found in bud when the lower ones have unfolded into blooms. Unlike most flowers, mine have no sepals. Now, as you know, it is the duty of sepals to protect the flower and hold it firmly together; so that when they are not present, some other way of protecting must be thought out. In my case, you will see that there are a great many red leaves called "bracts" surrounding my large group of flowers. These protect them while they are all tiny buds, and afterwards help to keep them safely attached to the stem to which they cling as tightly as they can. I am afraid, however, they would fall off easily, if it were not for the kind persistence of those bracts.

I can feel that cheeky Mountain Devil pricking me again. He is telling me I have been talking far too much, and had better stop straight away. So I shall take his advice as soon as I have sung my little song to you.

They call me proud and haughty
And arrogant and bold;
They say I am by nature
Intolerably cold.

But they are only teasing,
And in my heart I know
They'd sadly weep if ever
I went elsewhere to grow—

For often I have heard them
(When I have been so still
That they have thought me sleeping)
With admiration fill.

They've praised my height and grandeur,
And e'en my haughty stand.
They've said how proud to own me
Must be our sunny land.

I smile—But no-one sees me—
And gaily wink my eye,
Then innocently fix it
Upon the azure sky!

The Flannel Flower Fairy

(ACTINOTUS—type Helianthi)

It often amuses us flowers very much to hear the opinions that some mortals have of us. Of course, botanists are different, as they spend a great deal of their time studying us, and so are well acquainted with us and our habits.

But it always sounds very funny to us when people talk about the Arum Lily (which in reality is no lily at all) and the Asparagus Fern (which has nothing to do with a fern) and the petals of a Sunflower (which are not petals at all, but certain kinds of leaves called bracts) and again, the petals of the Flannel Flower, which are also just bracts. Then, there are many humans who think of me as belonging to the same family as the Daisy, whereas in reality, the Daisy's family (Compositae by name) and mine (Umbelliferae) are entirely different from one another.

Now, I suppose you will ask why it is that there are some flowers—both wild and cultivated—which are provided with these pretty, decorative bracts, whilst there are so many which haven't them at all. Well, I think you will be able to answer that question for yourselves if you try to imagine what a Daisy or a Zinnia or a Poinsettia or a Sunflower or a Flannel Flower would look like without its many bracts. In each case you will see how very unattractive those "centres" would appear if left all alone. And now, if you look carefully enough, you will see that what you had thought of merely as a part of one flower, is really many flowers all crowded together as closely as can be, forming what you call the "centre."

Of course, each little bloom is extremely small, so its petals are also very tiny and, to the casual observer, not important in the least. Neither are they noticeable to bees and other insects. And that is why those certain kind leaves named bracts have come to our assistance, making us visible to everyone. What we would do without them, I really do not know. I think we would be the most neglected flowers in the whole world, for we would never be visited by insects or admired by humans.

I think that my little readers all know why they call me a Flannel Flower, because they must all have seen me at least once or twice so far, and felt the soft woolliness of every part of me— from my green-tipped white bracts to my stems and leaves.

You see, just like the Wattle, who has already told you her story, and like very, very many other wildflowers, I have made my home not in gullies, but on the dry, rather barren hills, where there is little protection from the sun's rays. And as my Wattle friend has explained to you, sunbeams can be cruel as well as kind, and can steal from us the clear, cool water that thoughtful rains have given us to drink. That is why you will find a thick coat of wax on gum leaves, which does not allow the water to escape from them, and a thick woollen coat on my leaves, which not only protects them from the hear of sunbeams, but also from the hard, dry winds.

FLANNEL FLOWER.

(ACINOTUS—type helianthi)

Family: Umbelliferae. This name is given beacause the members of the family have their flowers arranged like the ribs of an umbrella.

Flowering seasons: Spring and summer.

Flowers: Very minute, and arranged like the ribs of an umbrella. They are surrounded by large white leaves (called "bracts") which are tipped with green. The outer flowers have no pistil—only five stamens. The inner ones have a pistil, which has two tubes called styles which can let the pollen grow through them all the way from the top of the pistil to the ovary at its bottom. All the flowers have five small sepals which are hairy.

The white bracts are woolly.

Leaves: Much divided in order that the plant might lose less water. As the leaves lose water more easily than any other part of the plant, the more divided they are, the less there is of them and therefore less water is lost. The leaves are wooly and grey-green in colour.

The stems are also covered with hairs.

This plant grows in dry, open country.

43

The Song of the Leopard Fairy

(DIURIS—type maculata)

I am such a fairy Orchid! Yes, of course, we all are! But some of my brothers and sisters and cousins become so much changed in the daytime from what they look like as fairies at midnight, that you really cannot think that they ever were fairies— but you only have to glance at me to see that I'm a fairy.

Just look how I cross my dainty legs and dance all day to the songs of birds and the buzz of bees and the rustling of grass— mortals would call them sepals; my brothers and sisters and aunts and uncles and cousins would call them sepals, but I am such a fairy Orchid, I must call them legs. Oh, I can't stop singing, I can't stop dancing, and this is the song I sing all day:

>Brilliant gold with freckles brown,
>>Open lands I love to grace:
>Shady nooks would not allow
>>Sunny beams to seek my face.

>'Midst the grasses tall I hide;
>>Humans' love I seldom hold,
>Yet my little flowers are formed
>>Out of Nature's purest gold.

>Frilly skirt and twinkle feet,
>>I upon the zephyrs dance
>By the roadside all the day
>>In a dreamy, fairy trance.

>By the roadside, on the hills,
>>Just a blossom in the light—
>When the world in silence sleeps,
>>Lovely fairy of the night!

LEOPARD ORCHID

(DIURIS—type maculata)

Family: Orchidaceae.

Flowering season: spring.

Flowers: Yellow in colour, usually much marked with brown. The lip (largest petal) is three-lobed. The two long, narrow, lower sepals cross each other. There are many different kinds of Diuris, and in plenty of them this crossing of the two lower sepals is seen.

There are usually from two to ten flowers on one stalk.

Leaves: Long, narrow and grass-like.

The Story of Little Blue Lobelia

(LOBELIA—type gibbosa)

(Told by MR. HONEYSUCKER)

Little Lobelia gibbosa was on the verge of jumping up and speaking to you this minute, but I, just a young Honeysucker, have flown along instead; and I have done this for the simple reason that I am so interested in this particular wildflower fairy.

As you can see by the name that people call me, I spend almost the whole of my life searching for honey. That is why I visit so many of the wildflowers which grow in Australia; for, you see, some of them are simply filled with honey. And, unless you have tasted it yourself, little human—unless you have actually sipped it, syrupy and sweet, from the very flowers in which it has been formed—I am sure you could never understand how delicious it is, or how I long for **more** as soon as I have tasted **some**, or how I devote my life to the finding of it.

But I am wandering away somewhat from the things I want to tell you.

In all my searches through plainlands, mountains and gullies, I do not remember ever having met a flower quite as fascinating as Lobelia. Of course, each one of them is very lovely in its own way, and I am fond of every one separately. Bur I suppose we must all have favourites. And so it is that every time I meet Lobelia I feel extra-specially happy.

At the magic hour, when I become a fairy bird I meet her as a fairy flower, and we walk and talk together a great deal, until the sky begins to put away its starry jewels and cast aside its heavy cloak of darkness. And because of this I have grown to know much more about her than the cleverest of humans do— although I am afraid I still know very little.

Lobelia is not as attractive to look at as are some of the other bush flowers. At the most, her plant is only about sixty centimeters high.

Her leaves are small, and not particularly graceful. Her flowers are also small and perhaps not very noticeable to unobservant eyes. But they are the colour of the sky at midnight, and to me they appear very lovely indeed. So much so, in fact, that whenever I see them, I cannot possibly resist them.

And the nearer I fly down to them, the more certain I begin to feel that there is a vast supply of honey awaiting me. Oh, how excited I grow then!

LOBELIA

(LOBELIA—type GIBBOSA)

Family: Campanulaceae. This family receives its name from a latin word meaning "bell." This is because so many of the flowers belonging to it are shaped like bells.

Flowering season: summer.

Flowers: Dark blue in colour. Five purplish sepals partly joined. Five petals which are not all the same in shape, and the bases of which are joined to form a small tube. The two upper ones are small, and curved backwards; the three lower ones are large and outspread, the middle one having three white lines on it which lead to the honey store. The flat blue stalks of the stamens serve to protect the honey, and the blue anthers form a tube which ends with tufts of hairs. The pistil's tubular 'style' also ends in hairs, and the stigma consists of two blue lobes.

Leaves: Not all alike in shape. The lower ones are wide and toothed; the upper ones narrow, and seldom toothed.

And how rapidly I continue my journey, until I am actually hovering about those dark blue flowers themselves.

But here is the puzzling part of the whole affair: it seems as if Lobelia, through a certain kind of perverseness that some flowers enjoy, is at the same time anxious and unwilling to entertain me. Of course, I know that she keeps her store of honey well concealed with those blue stamens of hers, so that it will not be stolen by the many insects who would like to run away with it. But all the same, it does seem rather bad behaviour towards me (an old friend) and at first I become considerably peeved.

I soon forget my troubles, however, when I find that in reality she is quite friendly towards me, and has done all she could to help me. For, upon her largest petal and leading to her precious honey store, there are three of the finest white lines. Now, for some unknown reason, I know what they mean and where they lead to, whereas all other birds and the great majority of insects never have the slightest idea of either. That is why there is always plenty of honey for me to enjoy. And you can be sure I do enjoy it.

I then say "thank you" and "good-bye" to the little blue flower. But as I do so, it happens without exception that I find on my feathers a tiny sprinkling of fine, yellow dust (which humans call "pollen," I believe). I look at it for a moment and wonder what it all means. The only thing I can be sure of is that Lobelia sprinkled it on me while I was busy a-honeying.

But after much wondering, I finally come to this decision: That it is a message of some kind that Lobelia wanted to send to one of her kinsfolk somewhere else in Bushland; and that she had treated me to particularly sweet honey so that I would be tempted to seek out another flower exactly like her, as soon as I had left her. Then, naturally, I would deliver the secret message when I had found the other, and all would be well.

What the message itself contains, however, I never can find out, although I guess and wonder about it a great deal. Perhaps it is an invitation to a Lobelia ball. Perhaps it is merely a piece of wildflower gossip. And perhaps it is a little message of love.

There is a flood of all-melodious songs,
A ceaseless harmony, and heaven's calm
That breathes upon my brow an airy charm;
A bubbling brook within which flowery throngs
Their beauty wistfully admire—and wrongs
Of men so far from this immortal balm
Of bushland peace appear. Each threat'ning harm,
 Here melts to naught, where God's own power belongs.

The Fairy of the Hilltops

(SPRENGELIA—type incarnata)

On the hilltops where the winds blow fiercely and where the grass is crisp and brown—that is where I grow, holding up staunchly my clusters of pale pink flowers and my long, stiff stems, covered all over by the sharply-pointed leaves that fold around them.

In springtime, when the birds sing sweetly and when dainty butterflies dance hither and thither, showing to the open plainlands their colourful wings, and carelessly sipping honey from all the flowers in turn, life is a happy and beautiful thing indeed.

But sometimes I unfold my petals before the warm spring comes, in the bleak winter. And then—Oh, the winds are fierce and destructive, the rains are speeding and cold, the sky is dark and dreary, and the hilltops are sad, for

There is no butterfly, no bird,
No sunshine warm and bright,
No melody that Summer heard,
Upon the mountain height.

The angry storm clouds sweeping by
O'ershade the hillsides steep,
And rush upon their wild, dark course,
Then sorrowfully weep!

SPRENGELIA—type incarnata

Family: Epacridaceae. To this family also belong the Heaths.

Flowering season: Spring, but sometimes even winter.

Flowers: Pale pink in colour and much crowded together. Five long, narrow petals. Five long, narrow, white sepals. There is a short corolla tube. The anthers are long and form a ring round the short pistil.

Leaves: Much crowded. Their bases fold round the stem, and each ends with a long, sharp point.

The Spurred Helmet Fairy

(CORYSANTHES—type aconitiflorus)

They call me a tiny helmet—
Ah yes, it is very true;
But there's something more than a helmet
About me, I think, don't you?

Oh, see me, a warrior fierce and bold,
With a sharp little sparkling eye,
And a most professional soldier's frown
And a shrill little soldier's cry!

Yes, though I am small, I have a very keen expression and character, as all my life, from the earliest moment I can remember, I have been a brave soldier, and it is because I used always to be crouching down in pursuit of the enemy that I simply got the habit, and at the present time no matter how straight I stand I am still quite tiny. But of course I don't mind, as I know my noble height has been sacrificed to nothing but kindness; for you know whom I mean by the "enemy," don't you? Why, caterpillars, snails, and all those tiny insects which creep into us and steal our honey without doing us the favour of carrying away some of our pollen in return. They give us a tremendous amount of extra work to do, making new honey to tempt the mosquitoes, beetles and birds, who are not nearly as selfish. So you can imagine how we long to be strong enough to chase them right away.

Day after day I stand on duty, adorned by my brilliant helmet, waiting for an opportunity to attack; thus you can see how it is I have such a sun-burnt appearance—even my helmet has gone a rusty sort of purple colour, whilst my only leaf, which is, indeed, larger than I and which is my constant companion, is not a fresh, clear green, but has become tinged with a dull mixture of purple, crimson, brown and yellow.

I suppose it is because this helmet of mine is so large when compared with the rest of me that people think I am nothing except it, and, would you believe it, they just tread right on top of me sometimes because they do not see me at all. Of course, I could hardly expect anything else, I suppose, when my plant consists of a tiny root, a big leaf, a short stem and a flower.

A long, long time ago when I was tall and commanding, I often used to ride a big, black horse at midnight and wear glittering spurs on my boots; but now I am so tubby, I think I may just roll off if I attempted to mount a horse again, so I stay safely on the ground all the time, mostly with my feet in dark, rich soil at the bottom of trees; but, can you guess what I have done?

SPURRED HELMET ORCHID.

(CORYSANTHES—type aconitiflorus)

Family: Orchidaceae.

Flowering season: winter.

Flowers: Purplish in colour. The largest sepal is shaped like a hood and ends at the base with two spurs.

Leaf: Lies flat on the ground, is roughly rounded in shape and large in comparison with the flower. Its colour is usually dark and purplish.

The whole plant is very small and short.

Well, I have fastened my spurs upon my helmet, partly to make it prettier, and partly to remind me of my glorious past.

Although I am very fond of my Orchid friends I have grown a little fearful these last few thousand years or so of getting crushed by mistake amongst the tremendous crowd of them which gathers together at spring-time, so I quietly open out my flower while they are still fast asleep beneath the ground, waiting for the warmer weather to come, and then I sink down just as quietly again into Mother Earth as they are opening out their little shoots and looking about them.

> They call me a tiny helmet—
> Ah yes, it is very true;
> But there's something more than a helmet
> About me, I think, don't you?

In pursuit of the enemy.

The Wild Flower Traveller

(CLEMATIS—type aristata)

They call me a trav'ller in Bushland—
The fairies and elfins and gnomes.
They look at me wand'ring the hillside
And say: "We have comfortable homes
Which we love and we prize and we care for,
While yonder white flower only roams!"

They speak of my habits with pity;
They watch as I come and I go;
They say that the pleasures of home-life
I "never—oh, never, could know."
They ask why I cannot be flower-like,
And settle in one place to grow?

But **I** love the call of adventure,
Its sound is like music to me.
I hear it, and then I must follow,
Wherever its dwelling may be—
Perhaps over large, frowning boulders,
Perhaps at the top of a tree.

Yet ne'er does my spirit grow older.
Through winter and summer I cling
Alike, and the forests I travel:
For autumn and winter **do** bring
A fluffy, grey beard to my features—
But blossoms return with the spring.

Oh, grand are those calls of adventure,
(Which many a flower cannot hear)
And grand is the spirit of roving
Whose song is so wild and so clear!
How could I regret that its music
Sounds ever more sweet in my ear?

CLEMATIS.

(CLEMATIS—type aristata)

Family: Ranunculaceae.

Flowering season: Spring and early Summer

Flowers: White coloured. Four sepals. Petals are absent. Many stamens, which are of varying lengths. To the end of each anther is attached a hair-like structure. The styles are short.

Leaves: Divided into three leaflets, about five cm long. They are toothed. The long leaf stalk twines round any support it can find.

Fruit: Looks like a parachute. It has one seed. It is easily carried on the wind by means of the long, feathery structures which have been formed from the styles.

57

The Heathy Parrot Pea Fairy

(DILLWYNIA—type ericifolia)

I have not always been a flower, you know—in fact, very few flowers have been, from the beginning of time, what they are now. Many thousands of centuries ago, I used to dance about the world on tip-toes as the prettiest butterfly you could imagine. My wings were not very large, nor even fancifully formed (as those of some butterflies are) but their colour was so bright that it was almost dazzling, and made them look just like pieces of the sky at sunset. Sometimes they were brilliant yellow, other times a rich orange. But always they were marked here and there with a deep, beautiful red.

The elves and fairies, of course, used to love me very much, and I used to love them. For one happy day we would frolic amongst the trees and ferns, then flutter up into the sky together; and when we began to feel a little hungry, we would all come down again and take a tiny sip of honey from the prettiest flower we could find.

But alas! At the end of that day which had been filled to the brim with joy and laughter, I would become so weary that I could not even smile at my fairy companions, and very soon my wings would fold gently around me, and I would die.

Now, this used to be a great sorrow to me, for life was so sweet and the sunshine so happy, and the whole wide world so beautiful.

Oh! how I used to think and think, as hard as I could, wondering what I might do to live just a little longer. The fairies thought, also; and the funny wee elves, putting on their considering caps, could only ever rest their chins in their hands and make wry faces, wrinkling their foreheads and screwing up their noses.

It was a sad problem indeed, and none of us, with all our efforts, could solve it. Then one day, as we were flying through the woods, we heard a very small, tearful voice. It seemed to come from somewhere near us, so we stopped suddenly and looked around for the speaker, hoping to bring it some comfort. And we did not take long in finding it, either, for it was quite a tall bush standing right beside us. Its leaves were rather small, fine and prickly. It had many long branches which drooped ever so slightly—and altogether it was a dainty little bush, which I immediately began to love.

"Oh," it cried plaintively, "I am sad and neglected. Every other plant around me is covered with sweet flowers which make it look so colourful

HEATHY PARROT PEA.

(DILLWYNIA—type ericifolia)

Family: Leguminosae. The group to which this flower belongs is called Papilionaceae, which comes from a Latin word meaning "butterfly." The group was given this name because of the likeness which its various flowers bear to the outspread wings of butterflies.

Flowering season: Spring and summer.

Flowers: They grow in loose clusters near the ends of branches, and are often orange-coloured with red markings. The largest petal is called the "standard." The two side ones are calledthe "wings," and the two small front ones, which are partly joined together, the "keel."

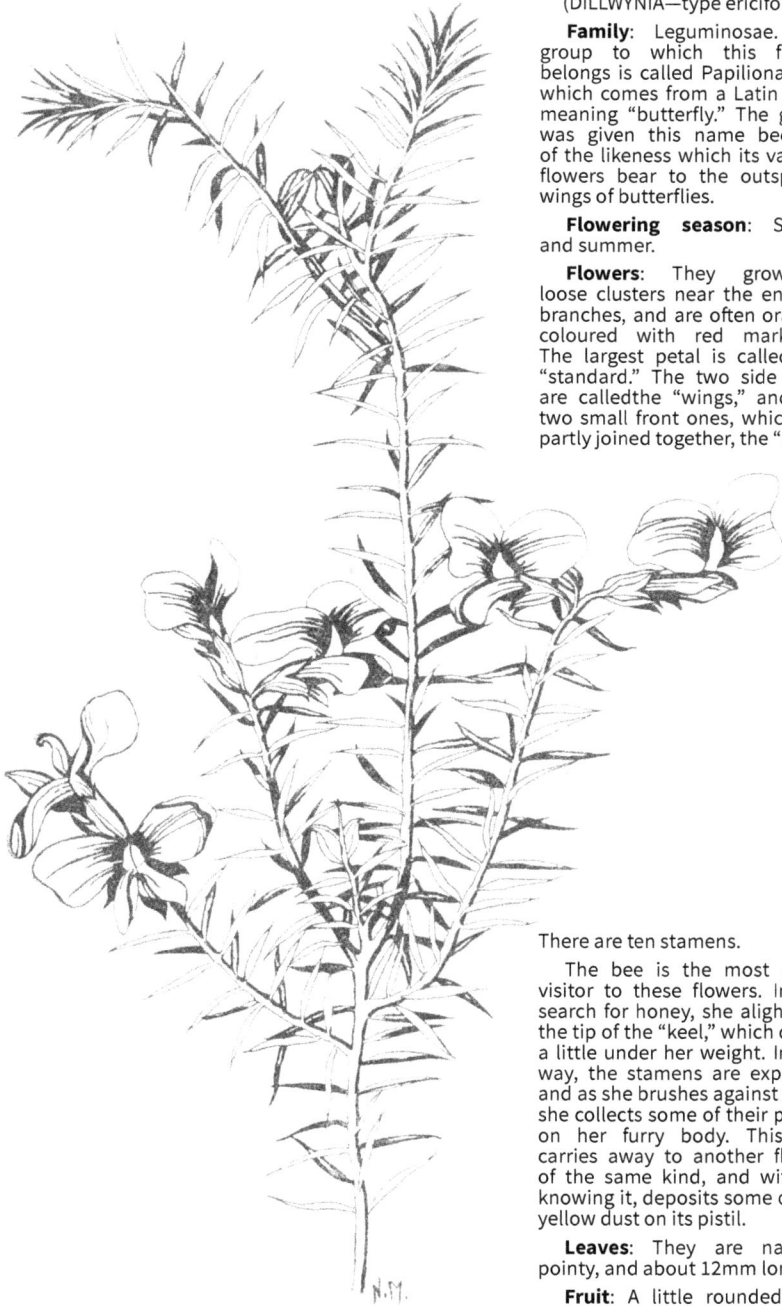

There are ten stamens.

The bee is the most usual visitor to these flowers. In her search for honey, she alights on the tip of the "keel," which drops a little under her weight. In this way, the stamens are exposed, and as she brushes against them she collects some of their pollen on her furry body. This she carries away to another flower of the same kind, and without knowing it, deposits some of the yellow dust on its pistil.

Leaves: They are narrow, pointy, and about 12mm long.

Fruit: A little rounded pod which contains two seeds.

N.M.

59

and gay; yet I have only stems and leaves. I do believe I am the only shrub in this big world without a flower upon it. Can nobody give me a flower for my very own, to keep and be proud of always?"

Immediately I heard these words, I knew that my opportunity had come, and that my life need never again last only for one short day. Quickly, I fluttered my way to the top of the longest branch, and there I nestled in amongst the small, green leaves— and became a flower!

The little bush nearly cried for joy—but it was no happier than I. "Look," it said excitedly to its companions, "I have a butterfly for a flower—a butterfly who is beloved of the fairies!"

And ever since then, I have heard mortals remark on the likeness I bear to the little winged creatures that often dance around me. Yet they never seem to realise the full extent of that likeness between us, or the fact that although I have the petals of a flower I have the soul of a butterfly.

Some people, referring to my colours, call me "Eggs and Bacon." Well, perhaps there is something in that too, although I cannot say I am very fond of it—and besides, that is really the popular name of one of my brothers,* whose petals are yellow for the most part with only the tiniest bit of red in them. The leaves of that plant are much closer together than mine, and the flowers are in more definite clusters. Also, it is a shorter shrub than I am, often not growing to any height worthy of mention.

> And so, a flower forever more
> I shall remain, and ever grow
> Where all day long the sun's bright rays
> Will round me glow!
>
> For it was by a craving strong
> That I became a little flower—
> And real desire within the heart
> Has magic power!

*DILLWYNIA floribunda.

"I've watched you now a full half-hour;
Self-poised upon that yellow flower
And, little Butterfly! indeed
I know not if you sleep or feed.
. . . .
This plot of orchard-ground is ours;
 My trees they are, my Sister's flowers,
Here rest your wings when they are weary;
Here lodge as in a sanctuary!
Come often to us, fear no wrong;
Sit near us on the bough!
We'll talk of sunshine and of song,
And summer days, when we were young;
 Sweet, childish days, that were as long
As twenty days are now."

—Wordsworth.

The Red Spider Flower Fairy

(GREVILLEA—type punicea)

Although people seem to think that my long, spreading red flowers look most attractive and are a great asset to the Australian bush, I do believe I am even more proud of the distinguished family to which I belong than of any flattering remark that I hear about myself personally.

Just the same as human families have names, so flower families have them also—and some of them look for all the world like Double Dutch. But mine is Proteaceae, which isn't bad at all.

You will see why I have called it a "distinguished" family when you know that only a few of its members are: the Waratahs, the Mountain Devils, the Parsley Plants, the beautiful Flame Wheel Tree of Queensland, the Bottlebrushes, and all the Grevilleas.

Now "Grevillea" is one of my names. But as I have to share it with a hundred and fifty-five other members of family Proteaceae, "punicea" has also been given to me. And that one name, at least, is exclusively mine.

We Grevilleas are a very hardy race; and some of us are ever so pretty, particularly Grevillea Banksii, who lives in Queensland. Some, naturally, are more delicate than others. But we have adapted ourselves to such varied conditions that you will find species of us growing in the sandy desert in the middle of this continent just as easily as others are able to grow in damper regions round the coast.

So that all together, I think you can now imagine what a fairyland of wonder it would be if every member of family Proteaceae could be encouraged to flower at the same time and in the same garden. Perhaps some day a kind magician or a fairy with a magic wand will make it possible. And then, I can almost see the throngs of people coming from far and wide to witness the fanciful sight.

It seems rather out of place now to talk about myself—so unimportant a unit of a glorious whole—does it not? But I think perhaps you would be interested to know that the under side of my leaves is covered with either silvery or bronze-coloured hairs which make them look very pretty.

Next time you are in the bush—no matter at what season of the year, for I flower nearly always—if you happen to pass my way and think you recognise me, you won't forget to look for those tiny hairs, will you? And if you do not find them—well, you will know you have come across one of my brother or sister Grevilleas instead.

RED SPIDER FLOWER.

(GREVILLEA—type punicea)

Family: Proteaceae.

Flowering season: Throughout the whole year.

Flowers: Red in colour, produced very close together in fairly large numbers, and arranged in pairs. Four united petals. The tube formed by these united petals is hairy inside. The four stamens, joined to the petals, are borne on the free petal lobes. The style is long, and the stigma is only released from the corolla tube when the pollen is mature.

Leaves: Oblong and about 4cm long. The underside is covered with bronze or silver coloured hairs.

Fruit: Pod-like, containing two seeds, and about 12mm long.

The Lament of the Spider Orchid

(CALADENIA—type Patersonii)

I used to be an ogre
In a great, ferocious cavern;
I used to trap the butterflies,
I used to eat the dragonflies,
I caught the fairies by surprise,
And Puck and Jack-o'-Lantern!

Once upon a time I was
The giant of all the spiders.
I used to prowl the woods by night
And carry elfins off in fright—
Oh, how they scattered at the sight
Of me—the giant of spiders!

But then there came a hero
With a white and sweeping feather!
He said he was a fairy knight,
We had a long and mighty fight,
And when I was defeated quite
He said to me in accent slight:
"What very pleasant weather!"

Then, waving over me his wand,
Declared: "You heartless midnight glider!
You'll be a flower forever more—
No longer fairies frighten, for
You're nothing greater after all
Than what the whole wide world will call
An 'artificial spider'!"

SPIDER ORCHID.

(CALADENIA—type patersonii)

Family: Orchidaceae.

Flowering season: spring.

Flowers: Usually cream-coloured, with deep red markings. The petals and sepals (except the "labellum") are very long and pointy. Sometimes one flower measures 23 cm across. There are two or three blooms on the one stem, although sometimes there is only one. The "labellum" is fringed, and tipped with red.

Leaves: Long and grass-like. They are hairy, as are the stems. The plant is about 40cm high.

The Dwarf Apple Fairy
(ANGOPHORA—type cordifolia)

Looking at my large, full clusters of creamish-coloured flowers, you could easily imagine me to be a gum tree. But the fact that when quite grown-up I am still only a shrub would make you think otherwise. And together with this difference between us there are many more—for instance, gum leaves are smooth and are sometimes (especially when young) shiny. But my leaves have rather a dull appearance always, and the baby ones are covered with a thick coat of hairs. Then also, they are arranged in pairs opposite to one another along my stems, whereas those of the gum trees are not.

The leaves of a very near relation of mine* are more similar to the Eucalyptus, being long and ending with a point. But mine are short, and rounded at the tip.

Even in the flowers themselves there are differences to be found. You all know quite well the little lid which covers the gum blossom bud, but which is pushed off as the stamens press harder and harder against it in their effort to greet the happy sunshine. Well, this tiny lid is really the five sepals of the flower joined together. My sepals, however, are not joined all the way up; they are separated from one another at the tips and, while my flowers are still in bud, can be seen folded right over and protecting them. They also are covered with a coat of hairs which are red in colour. This coat, as you can imagine, makes my buds very pretty and cosy-looking. Then, when they unfold into flowers, my bush seems overladen with their wealth of cream-coloured stamens.

I have no petals which could attract insects to my flowers, so those stamens not only have to hold the pollen, but to make themselves attractive as well. They never feel imposed upon, however, as both tasks give them the greatest enjoyment. There are many of them in each flower, and they are arranged around a little cup from the centre of which grows the short pistil. This cup also holds the most delicious honey; so I hardly need tell you that when my bush is in bloom, it is simply crowded with bees, beetles and other insects—all of them having a feast of honey.

Of course, there are many kinds of Native Apple trees, and I am the smallest of them—as you can guess from my name, Dwarf Apple. But

* ANGOPHORA lanceolatus.

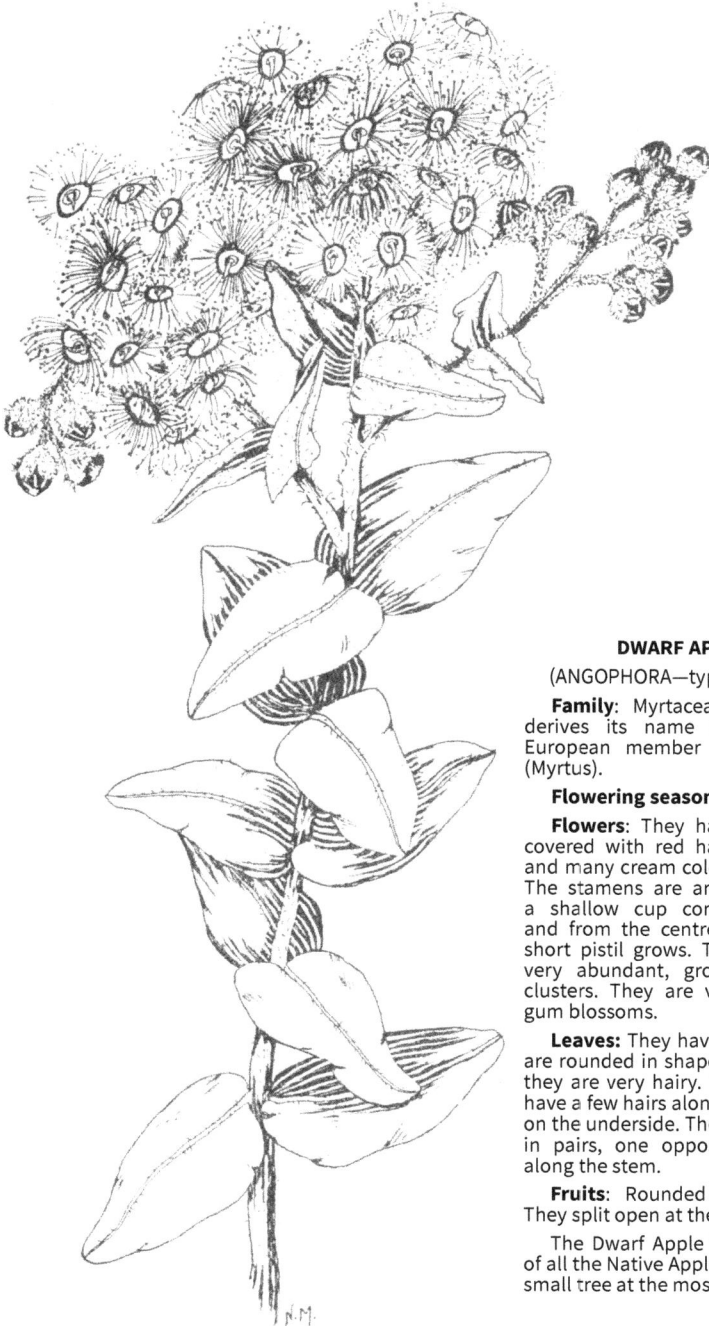

DWARF APPLE.

(ANGOPHORA—type cordifolia)

Family: Myrtaceae. This family derives its name from its only European member — the Myrtle (Myrtus).

Flowering season: summer.

Flowers: They have five sepals covered with red hairs, no petals, and many cream coloured stamens. The stamens are arranged around a shallow cup containing honey and from the centre of which the short pistil grows. The flowers are very abundant, growing in great clusters. They are very much like gum blossoms.

Leaves: They have no stalks and are rounded in shape. When young, they are very hairy. The older ones have a few hairs along their mid-ribs on the underside. They are arranged in pairs, one opposite the other, along the stem.

Fruits: Rounded and cup-like. They split open at the top.

The Dwarf Apple is the smallest of all the Native Apples, being only a small tree at the most.

I have often heard it said that I am the favourite amongst humans because of my very shortness, which makes my large and abundant flowers so easy to reach.

The name by which botanists call me (Angophora) come from two Greek words, one meaning "cup," and the other "carrying"—and refers to my cup-like fruits.

Now, we Native Apples do not grow all over Australia—only in the eastern part of it; and I cannot live comfortably outside New South Wales. But there are so many likenesses between us that you need only be familiar with one of us to be able to recognise the rest of us. I think you know me fairly well now, don't you? You must just remember that all my brothers and sisters are taller than I am, and that some of them have pointy leaves, and you will easily know them wherever you see them.

We are proud of the family likeness we bear to Eucalyptus flowers, for they are such distinguished relations, don't you think?

"'Now what is the flower, the ae first flower
        Springs either on moor or dale;
And what is the bird, the bonnie, bonnie bird,
        Sings on the evening gale?'—

'The primrose is the ae first flower
        Springs either on moor or dale;
And the thistlecock is the bonniest bird
        Sings on the evening gale.'"

—From "Proud Lady Margaret" (an old Scotch ballad)

The Story of the Wild Violet Fairy

(VIOLA—type hederacea)

There was a little creek in Fairyland long, long ago—a little sparkling creek that seemed to be made of all the jewels in the world melted together; and unlike many of its brothers and sisters throughout the world, it flowed along its tiny, narrow path as silently as the moon rises up on the starry sky.

There were no rocks or pebbles in its way to hinder it—nothing whatsoever—and when you looked into it, you could see only reflections. Sometimes, you would wonder what there existed below them, at the very bottom of the creek; and after looking into it as deeply as you could for a long time, you would decide that it was simply reflections all the way down.

Well, we fairies and elves used to love this tiny brooklet very much indeed. We used to sit beside it and tell it all our secrets and ask its advice on many things. But, far from being of a talkative nature, it always remained perfectly silent and was never once known to answer a single question or make the slightest remark.

So we used to flutter about it, and have jumping contests over it until the hills and valleys of Fairyland would resound with our merriment. Then, when we were too tired to play, we would sit down again on its banks, dangling out feet in it and chattering together the whole afternoon.

Of course, when night began to fall, all the fairies would gradually fly away—some to their homes, others to parties, and still others to glow-worm lighted ballrooms.

But mostly, I would stay behind, and very soon I would be left quite alone on the brink of the sparkling water (now even more beautiful than before, because the moon and countless stars were reflected in it.)

There was nothing in the whole of Fairyland that I loved as much as my silent and beautiful friend. And, although it never once spoke to me, I used to feel that it, too, was fond of me; for in winter-time, when all the elves would be shivering with cold, I would go down to the little creek, and when I dangled my feet in it, it would flow over them with tingling warmth. And when it was hot summer-time, it would flow over them with icy cold.

But after many, many years of fairy-happiness had passed by, something sad and terrible happened: humans began to live on Earth, and to growl at and hate each other. They seemed to hate all Nature as well (as far as I

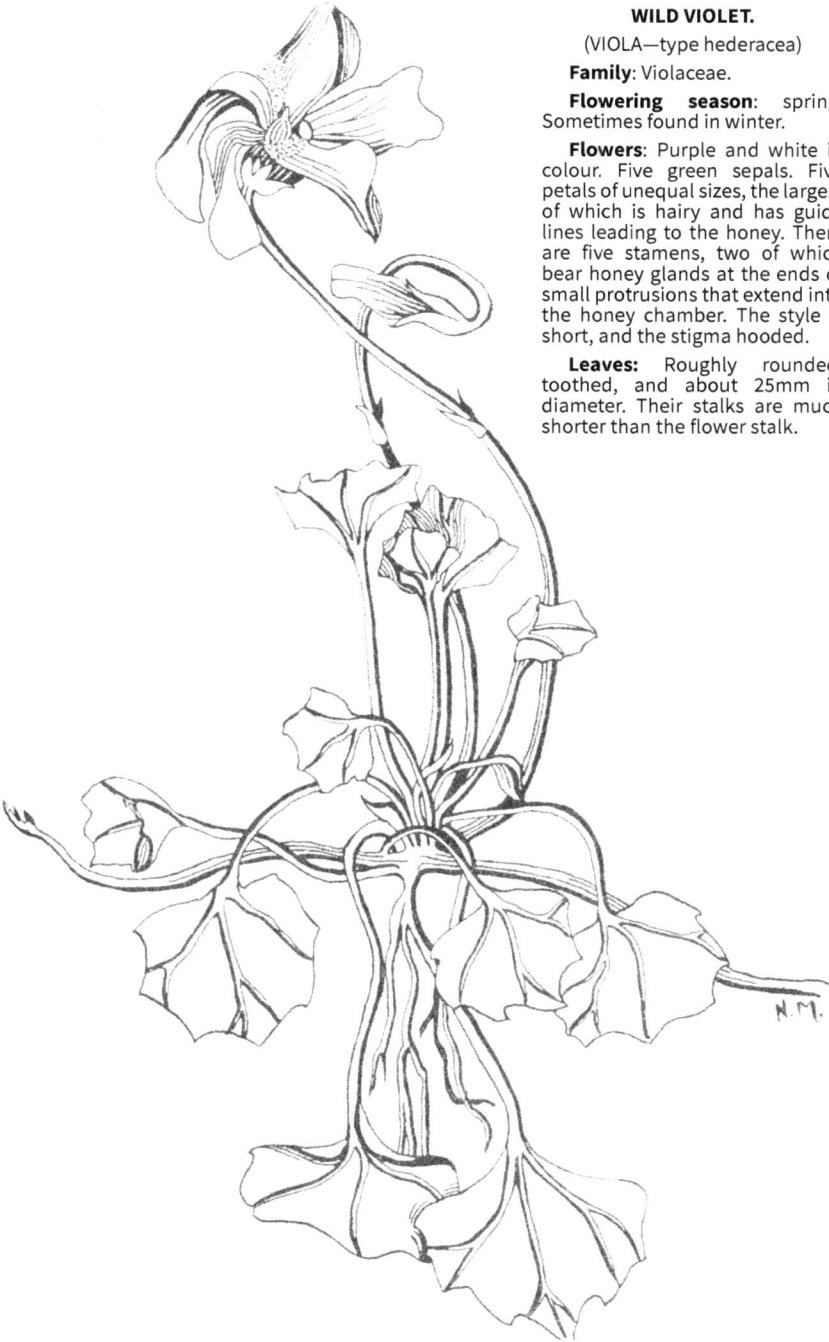

WILD VIOLET.

(VIOLA—type hederacea)

Family: Violaceae.

Flowering season: spring. Sometimes found in winter.

Flowers: Purple and white in colour. Five green sepals. Five petals of unequal sizes, the largest of which is hairy and has guide lines leading to the honey. There are five stamens, two of which bear honey glands at the ends of small protrusions that extend into the honey chamber. The style is short, and the stigma hooded.

Leaves: Roughly rounded, toothed, and about 25mm in diameter. Their stalks are much shorter than the flower stalk.

could see) for they started straight away to cut down our lovely trees, to tread upon our mossy carpets, to root out our ferns and flowers, to break through our very haunts, to tear away our tiny bridges of vines and creepers; for, you see, the Earth that you know now was Fairyland before.

Oh, it was so cruel and horrible that we fairies could live no longer in the world which had been our own for thousands of ages.

There was a wonderful country far beyond the sunset, though, as yet untouched by mortal hands. And that was where we all decided to go, and to make new homes, where none could hurt us.

But it was ever so hard to part with all the magic, secret haunts we had loved. And I felt that I could **never** part with my little voiceless creek. However, the day came at last when I knew I would have to depart; and I went sorrowfully down to the ferny banks to say farewell. But as I leaned down over them to kiss them, two large tears gathered in my eyes and fell into the crystal waters. Then instantly, as if those tears had awakened some long-pondered thought into sound, I heard a murmuring voice coming to me from the very depths of the creek of reflections:

"Violet, little Violet, stay with me. Do not leave me. I would dry away into the earth forever if you say good-bye to me. Turn yourself into a flower bearing the same name as your name and the same colour as your eyes and your pretty frock—and wander along my banks forever!"

And that was exactly how Wild Violets first began to grow, little human, and how they will grow until the end of time, sitting upon the banks of gurgling rivulets and gazing into their depths the whole day long.

"A violet by a mossy stone,
Half hidden from the eye;
    —Fair as a star, when only one
Is shining in the sky."

—Wordsworth.

The Rose Heath Fairy
(BAUERA—type rubioides)

Here, on the mainland of Australia, I am quite a harmless little plant, gently wandering about amongst the ferns that grow deep down in dark green gullies. But in Tasmania, I am not nearly as well behaved, and consequently people do not think very kindly of me; for there, I twine in and out and around things so much—my rambling wiry plant becoming so tangled and interfering so much in the affairs of other plants—that even humans simply cannot make their way through me, and call me a terrible nuisance as well as other things that are not over complimentary.

However, I do not really mind such treatment and so, towards those who are calling me gruff names, I turn my little pale-pink flowers, which always have the art of looking innocent and sweet.

And in this way, I mostly win the good favour of mortals who are kind; although the less gentle ones still continue to grumble and to stamp their feet upon me just as if I had never tried to appeal to them at all. Such is the manner of mortals.

Well, although I am not entirely uncared for, neither am I, as a general rule, cherished amongst the wildflowers of Australia.

When this sorrow becomes more than I can bear, I hold up my pretty rose-like flowers as high as I can and remind people that the beautiful and famous Christmas Bush* belongs to exactly the same family as I do, and therefore can be considered my very near relation. It is only reflected glory on my part, I suppose, but it certainly does win me much respect, and I lift my head up just a wee bit higher on account of it.

> A little Rose Heath white or pink,
> Who flowers when all the bird-choirs sing,
> Who flowers when all the world is young,
> Who flowers in summer and in spring.
>
> A Rose Heath bloom, so frail of form,
> So delicate and sweet of hue,
> That none would think its tangling stems
> Could ever vex or worry you!

* CERATOPETALUM gummiferum.

ROSE HEATH.

(BAUERA—type rubioides)

Family: Cunoniaceae.

Flowering season: Spring and summer.

Flowers: Pink in colour. They have four to ten reddish sepals, four to ten large free pink petals, and many stamens.

Leaves: Arranged opposite to one another. They have no stalks. Each consists of three leaflets which are oblong in shape, and toothed. Each leaflet is about 12mm long.

N.M.

The Hyacinth Orchid Fairy

(DIPODIUM—type punctatum)

'Tis true that all the fairies say I am terribly vain and tease me any amount about it. Well, don't you think I have something to be vain about with a delicate summer frock of pink flower-satin, made in dainty flounces, and a dear little petal with a fur coat, and such a majestic height?

Perhaps you are wondering how I happen to possess those tiny dark pink spots all over my petals, are you? It is rather a mischievous story accomplished by an elf who thought I was really far too conceited, so I think you would enjoy it.

A little elf in search of fun
One time, as day had just begun,
Stole forth from Fairyland to where
The giants of Fire had built their lair;
And soon he found his little plot
Was one intolerably hot.
Still, round the flames he wildly flew,
For somewhere there he right well knew
There lived, our sky-roof to adorn
The rosy colour of the morn.
At last a secret nook he eyed,
And peering in it, he espied
A monstrous pot of rich, pink paint;
And as but little of the saint
Within him dwelt, that naughty elf
Gave brush and paint-pot to himself:
He filled an acorn to the brim,
Then, lest the giants should capture him,
Flew quickly down upon the earth,
His little spirits full of mirth;
And fluttered round the woods till he,
In giggling merriment, met me;
And on my face so free from taint,
He sprinkled all his stolen paint.
Then somewhat shy, the guilty elf
To Fairyland betook himself!
And hence those spots of darker pink—
They're rather pretty, don't you think?

HYACINTH ORCHID.

(DIPODIUM—punctatum)

Family: Orchidaceae.

Flowering season: Summer, autumn, and sometimes winter.

Flowers: Usually pink in colour and spotted. The lip is small and furry. There are many flowers on the one stalk, which is brown in colour.

Leaves: Only tiny brown scales at the base of the stem which bears the flowers.

Roots: Thick. Many a plant which steals food from another plant is a "fungus." However, not every fungus is a thief, and it is one of this kinder sort that lives with the roots of the Hyacinth Orchid.

N M

The Trigger Plant Fairy

(STYLIDIUM—type graminifolium)

It is more or less unusual to see any sharp, rapid movement in flowers. Of course, what goes on at the magic hour is quite another story; but it is a secret that humans can never know. So it is that in the minds of even the cleverest mortals we, the many inhabitants of Flower Kingdom, are looked upon as unintelligent, thoughtless little beings with life and very little else.

Well, as I come under the laws of the Flower King, I cannot disclose what goes on at the magic hour; but I **can** say this; that there are many, many things which mortals never dream of, and that even "feelingless" objects have souls.

Now, I am one of the few wildflowers that keep a wee bit of their liveliness even during daylight hours. My Orchid friend, Ptetostylis longifolia is another, and as she has been given the same names for the parts of her flower as I have, and as we both do very nearly the same thing, the story she tells will also explain to you a portion of mine. But unlike her, mosquitoes very seldom even come near me, and my "column" instead of my "labellum" is responsible for the "springing."

It is when I receive a visit from the little black bush bee that my column prepares itself for action. And this is just how it happens: Ms. Bee comes flying along looking for honey, and when she sees me, with my four outspread, pink petals, she dives down head first right on top of me.

Now, she always lands exactly opposite my column (which is made up of my stamens and pistils all in one), and once there, she finds that there are tiny spikes on all my petals, which I have put there to guide her in the right direction. This direction is "tight" not only for her (because it leads her to the honey) but also for me (because it enables me to sprinkle her with pollen.)

Well, to continue the story, Ms. Bee goes clumsily forward until she runs, again head first, into my column. When this happens she gets quite a shock, for that mischievous young column quickly springs over on her back and makes her prisoner.

Needless to say, she struggles very hard to free herself, and while she does so I have a wonderful opportunity to dust her all over with pollen.

Then at last she escapes, feeling very hot and very bothered— as you

TRIGGER PLANT.

(STYLIDIUM—type graminifolium)

Family: Stylidiaceae.

Flowering season: Spring, summer, autumn, and sometimes early winter.

Flowers: Pink in colour. There are five petals, the bases of which are united in a short tube. Four of them are large and outspread, each with a small outgrowth which guides the pollinating insect to the honey. The fifth petal ("labellum") is curved back, and is smaller than the other four. It has two outgrowths which guide the column back after it has "sprung". This "springing" is caused by the insect, whose head comes into contact with it. It springs on his back, and as he struggles to escape he becomes sprinkled with pollen.

There are usually many flowers on the tall stem. The sepals (joined to form a tube), the short flower stalks, and the under surface of the four outspread petals are covered with sticky hairs.

Leaves: Grass-like, and growing in a tuft, from the centre of which the stalk bearing all the flowers arises.

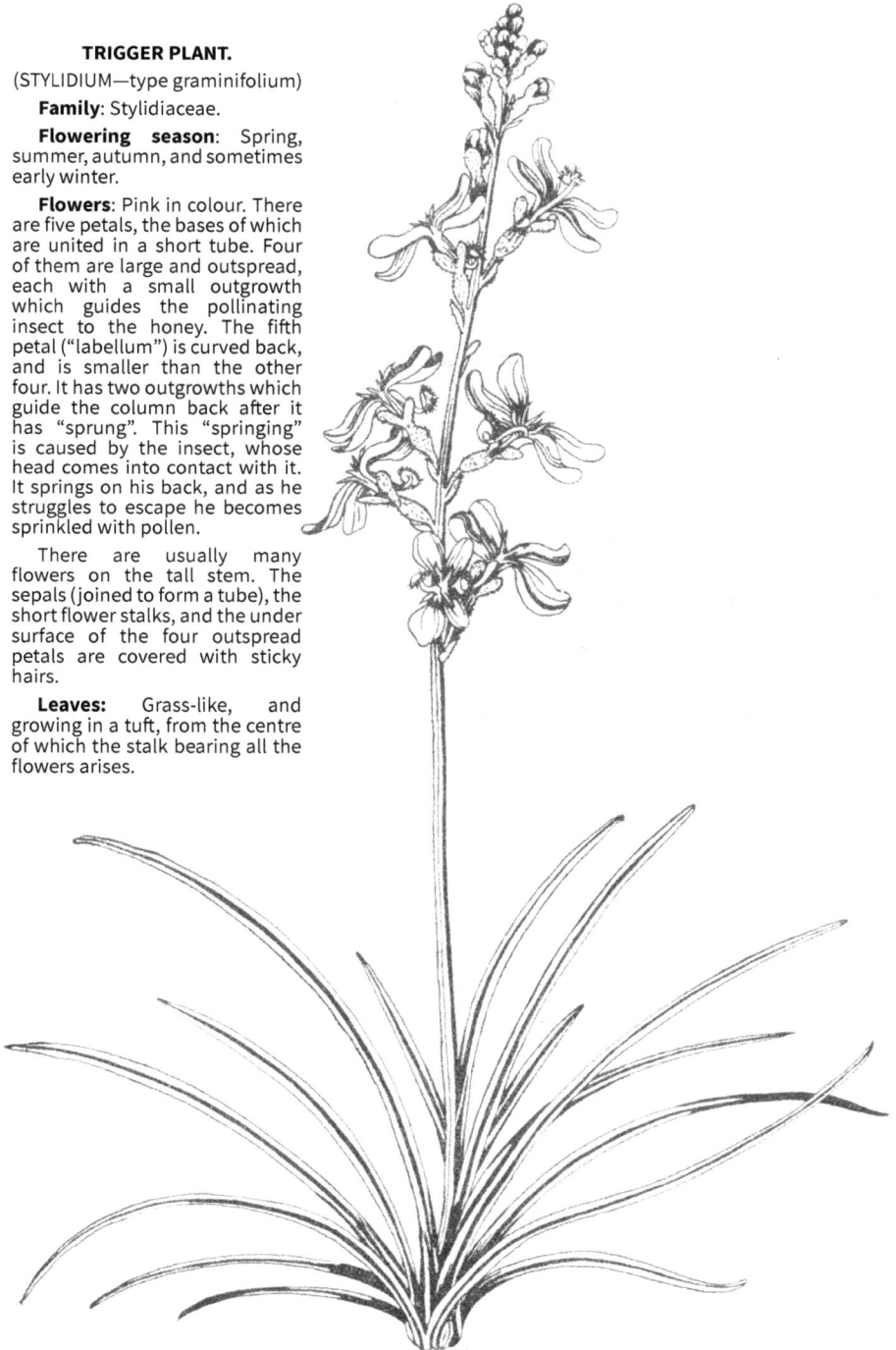

can well imagine. And while she is flying away as fast as her wings will carry her, I call out to her, in flower-language:

"Good-bye, Ms. Bush Bee, and I hope you enjoyed your honey!"

This makes her even more disgruntled. She mutters a lot of things to herself, and vows she will never go near any flower of my likeness again. But somehow or other she does; and at times she even comes back to me myself, without knowing it. She is a nice little lady, and never one to stay offended very long.

Yes, like my Orchid friend Pterostylis longifolia, I also have a labellum, and although it is not the chief actor in the small drama I have just related, it **has** got its own little part to play; for on its upper edge there are two more tiny spikes, whose duty it is to guide my column back into its position again, after it has finished teasing poor, harmless Ms. Bee.

Of course, when insects are having a day at home and are refusing to visit me, my column has nothing to do, and so remains quite still and sometimes (I fear) goes to sleep. Also, it is inclined to feel a bit sleepy when the day is cool and damp instead of warm and dry.

And now, just one more thing I must tell you, which is to look at my small, stiff sepals, and the underside of my petals, and the short stalks which attach each of my flowers to my main stem (or peduncle). If you look closely enough, you will see that they are covered with the tiniest and stickiest hairs which very soon chase away those naughty insects that have planned to come into my flower through the back door and steal my valuable honey.

Ariel:

       "Where the bee sucks there suck I:
       In a cowslip's bell I lie;
       There I couch when owls do cry.
       On the bat's back I do fly
       After summer merrily.
    Merrily, merrily shall I live now
    Under the blossom that hangs on the bough."

                           —Shakespeare

The DandelionFairy

(TARAXACUM—type densleonis)

Happy little carefree flower
By the roadside growing—
Children love to see my blooms
In the sunshine glowing,
Yet that precious, brilliant gold
(Which all people may behold)
Never, since the world began,
Has been craved by any man!

Fluffy, snowy "puff-o'clocks"
By the roadside growing—
Children love those "parachutes"
In the breezes blowing.
What a happy little band!
Are they bound for Fairyland?
Are they fairies in disguise,
Flying 'gainst the azure skies?

It is in lawns and at the borders of flower-beds (where I know very well I should not be) that I, a member of the famous Daisy family, like best to live. You see, although grown-up humans are hardly ever interested in me, I am interested in them. I do enjoy studying their various gestures and facial expressions. This study is more enlightening than you may imagine, for when the most even-tempered man comes across me in the middle of his favourite flower-bed, I have the pleasure of seeing him in a mood quite different from his usual one.

Little children are different, though, and are always delighted when they find me by the roadside or in meadows. They pick as many of my flowers as their hands will hold, then sit down and make "daisy chains" of them. Perhaps there is nothing I love more than to see children twining me around their heads or shoulders and, thus adorned, skipping merrily home.

The butterflies also are my friends; they flutter around me and lazily take a sip of honey now and then. They are beautiful, idle, posing little creatures, so different from the buzzing, ever active bees that, with a very business-like air, visit one flower after another, then immediately fly away, not wasting a single moment. Beetles also come to me sometimes. They are certainly not as dainty as butterflies or as industrious as bees. What **they** like is a long rambling talk—and once they start, I never can stop them, or get a word of my own in, either, for that matter. Then there are the flies—the

DANDELION.

(TARAXACUM—type densleonis)

Family: Compositae. This is a very large family to which the daisies also belong. The Dandelion and Daisy, however, belong to different groups of the family.

Flowering season: Spring and summer, although it is to be found flowering in the other two seasons as well.

Flowers: Bright yellow in colour. There are very many flowers in each head—usually more than a hundred and fifty. Those on the outside open first. There are five joined petals, and the five stamens form a tube around the pistil. The end of the pistil grows out beyond the tube, however, and is forked. The sepals are represented by a ring of hairs near the base of the flower. The Dandelion is visited by many insects, such as bees, beetles, flies, butterflies, and others.

Leaves: Usually long, and they are not all the same in shape. There are many divisions in them, but these do not extend in as far as the mid-rib. They end with a point; the lower ones lie flat along the ground.

The flower stems are hollow, and sometimes attain a height of 45 cm.

Fruits: Each fruit contains one seed and ends with a little point. At the top of it there is a very fine stalk, and at the top of this stalk there is a ring of fine white hairs.

These hairs act as a parachute, helping the tiny fruit to be carried easily by the wind. It is called the "pappus."

Dandelion plants are so numerous and are to be found in so many places because of the enormous number of fruits that are produced on each head, and because of the ease with which these are carried away to different parts.

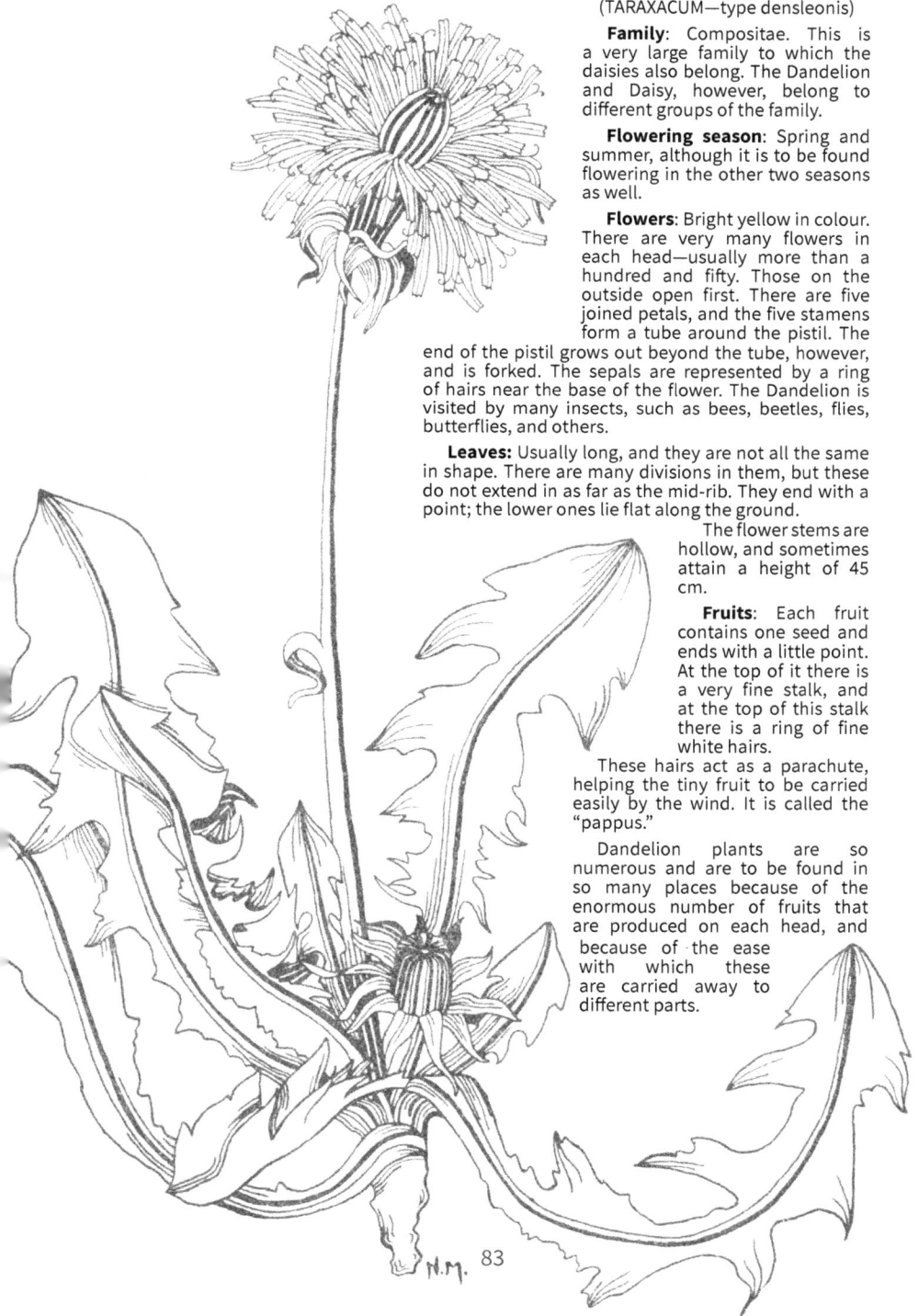

N.M. 83

poor despised little flies. They always seem rather fond of me—I suppose because I am a poor, despised little weed.

My native home is not Australia—it is Europe and Asia. But I am able to live in any country at all, as long as it is not too hot in summer or too cold in winter.

Now, some flowers find travelling difficult, and so cannot visit other countries of the world with ease. But in this I am very fortunate, as Nature has provided each of my seeds with a white, fluffy "parachute." It looks frail enough, I know, but it enables my seed to travel for great distances over both land and sea, if necessary. The slightest breeze is sufficiently powerful to carry it away with its precious little cargo. Of course, when the seed finds herself in a piece of ground that she likes, she decides at once to settle down. The wee "parachute" soon falls away from her, so that the wind will not be able to carry her away any more—and before very long, that seed has grown into a new Dandelion plant. That is why the gardener feels so hostile to "puff-o'clocks"; for as he cannot chase and catch every "parachute" he sees, he knows that in a short time he will have to go about pulling out ever so many more Dandelion plants than he had dreamed of. Poor gardener! Although I am loyal to myself (as we all are) I cannot help feeling sorry for him sometimes.

But again I discover that I am not neglected by the goodwill of all humans— even when "parachutes" appear. Perhaps now, more than ever before, children love me. They tell the time by me (as fairies do) and watch the flight of the tiny travellers until, on a windy day, they can be seen no longer.

Of course, you know that each of them is formed from a separate flower; and as every Dandelion "flower" (as you call it) is really composed of over a hundred and fifty tiny yellow blooms, the number of "parachutes" is very great indeed. No wonder the gardener feels worried when he sees them!

What a happy little band!
Are they bound for Fairyland?
Are they fairies in disguise,
Flying 'gainst the azure skies?

"When rosy May comes in wi' flowers,
To deck her gay, green-spreading bowers,
Then busy, busy, are his hours,
    The gardener wi' his paidle."*
The crystal waters gently fa',
The merry birds are lovers a',
The scented breezes round him blaw—
    The gard'ner wi' his paidle."

—Burns

*Hoe.

The Native Fuchsia

(EPACRIS—type longiflora)

Unlike most wildflowers, whose favourite seasons are spring and summer, my favourite of the whole four is winter. Of course, I do stay in Bushland sometimes to see the arrival of beautiful Lady spring. But to see my own little red and white bell-shaped flowers shedding a tiny splash of colour through the forest when it is otherwise sad and cold is really a great enjoyment to me.

Sometimes I visit the open plains, and say, "How do you do?" to the shrubs and grasses. But mostly it is the moist, shady gullies that I haunt, and the rocks around waterfalls. There, my long and somewhat untidy little shrub straggles about aimlessly, and my plentiful flowers hang down gracefully side by side, dreaming and nodding together and sometimes blowing back and forth more violently in the strong, cold wind.

If you were to listen ever so carefully as you were going past me, and if your ears had just a little magic in them, perhaps you would hear me sing:

> Little bells of red and white,
> Swaying on a dainty stem,
> Winter raindrops on us fall—
> It is we who welcome them:
> Other flowers were made so shy
> That they fear a clouded sky.
>
> And, when autumn days have flown
> Where the weary seasons go,
> All the blossoms fade away,
> Saying they refuse to grow
> While the winds are blowing strong
> Past their petals all day long.
>
> But I love to feel my flowers
> Shuffled roughly to and fro.
> It is then that fairy ears,
> List'ning where the wild winds blow,
> From the mossy, ferny dells
> Hear the tinkling of my bells—
> Ringing, ringing day and night,
> Little bells of red and white!

NATIVE FUCHSIA.

(EPACRIS—type longiflora)

Family: Epacridaceae.

Flowering season: Winter and early spring.

Flowers: Red and white in colour; sometimes pale pink or even all white. Five green sepals. Five joined petals with free lobes. Five stamens joined to the petals, and a long pistil. A number of small bracts surround each flower. The blooms are crowded, and grow singly on short stalks arising from those parts where the leaves are attached to the stem.

Leaves: Crowded, small, pointed and heart-shaped.

87

The Burr Buttercup Fairy

(RANUNCULUS—type lappiaceus)

Little golden buttercup nodding to and fro,
Spring and early summer—that is when I grow.
A tiny bag of honey upon each petal lies,
To which come all the busy bees and all the butterflies.
They tell me lovely stories of strange and wondrous things
That in the world are happ'ning. You see, they all have wings—
And while I have to live in soil and dream the hours away,
I always see them soar and whirl and dance the live-long day.
At times I wish that I could change my petals gold for wings;
That I could pass the garden wall and meet those wondrous things.
But no! My fate is not to roam—
The Mother Earth is e'er my home!
For while the world was very young the sun forgot, one day,
That when the twilight came his beams must all be tucked away.
He left **me** out, and all night long I scanned the forest wild
Until the fairies found me—a little sunlight child.
They said that golden beams, once lost, could ne'er espy again
The magic pathway to the sky. They said I'd search in vain.
And that is why, so long ago,
In woodlands I began to grow—
That on those days when dark, grey clouds obscured the sun's
        warm glow,
I might remain, one brilliant light, a-nodding to and fro!

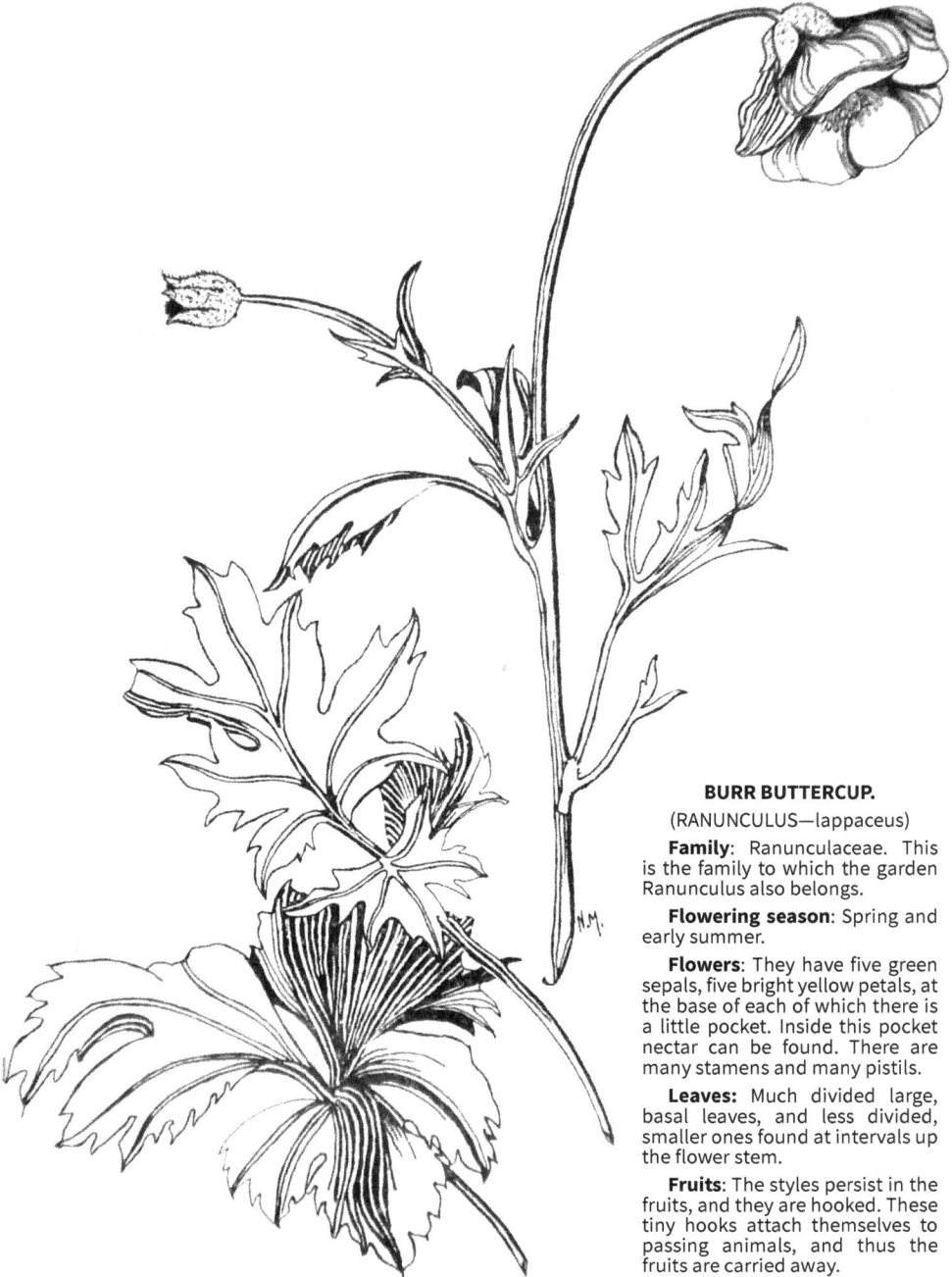

BURR BUTTERCUP.

(RANUNCULUS—lappaceus)

Family: Ranunculaceae. This is the family to which the garden Ranunculus also belongs.

Flowering season: Spring and early summer.

Flowers: They have five green sepals, five bright yellow petals, at the base of each of which there is a little pocket. Inside this pocket nectar can be found. There are many stamens and many pistils.

Leaves: Much divided large, basal leaves, and less divided, smaller ones found at intervals up the flower stem.

Fruits: The styles persist in the fruits, and they are hooked. These tiny hooks attach themselves to passing animals, and thus the fruits are carried away.

The Story of the Christmas Bell Fairy

(BLANDFORDIA—type nobilis)

(Told by MR. HONEYSUCKER)

There is a wonderful spirit of love and kindness which fills the very air at Christmas time, and of which that lovely month of December is formed (I sometimes think). Some people like to call it Santa Claus, others St. Nicholas, others the Three Kings who brought the beautiful gifts to the little child Jesus.

But no matter what one calls it, it still remains; and nearly everyone in the whole wide world feels it. Those who do **not** feel it are unfortunate people indeed.

The fairies, of course, love every name that mortals like to give it. But for themselves, and in Fairyland, it is always known as the Spirit of Giving; for as the end of the year draws near you will notice that everyone wants to give to someone else.

And it is not only humans who feel this Spirit of Giving. It is all the fairies and elves and goblins and gnomes as well. But whereas mortals think only of other mortals, fairies think of the great extensive woodlands—and over them they wave their magic wands of giving.

Then suddenly, the bush awakens into the loveliest blooms, and people, going by, sometimes pick large bunches of them and take them back to their homes in the city, saying:

"Fancy! What glorious Christmas bush!"

And some, whose attention is fastened upon the ground as well as on tall trees, find certain little red and yellow bells, which they also pick and carry home with them. These being another gift of the kind fairies to the Australian bush.

Now, I am really fond of Christmas Bells, that nod together lazily in the summer sunshine, and droop their graceful heads, and whisper secrets to each other which no one ever knows except themselves. I love to flutter all around them and try (without any success) to hear what they are saying. And I love to sip their honey, and feel their soft pollen on my feathers—their pollen which is so delicate that they **must** droop their heads towards the ground in order to protect it from the dampness of the air.

Afterwards, however, when the little case that holds their seeds grows so fast that it is longer than the petals and sepals themselves, then the flowers

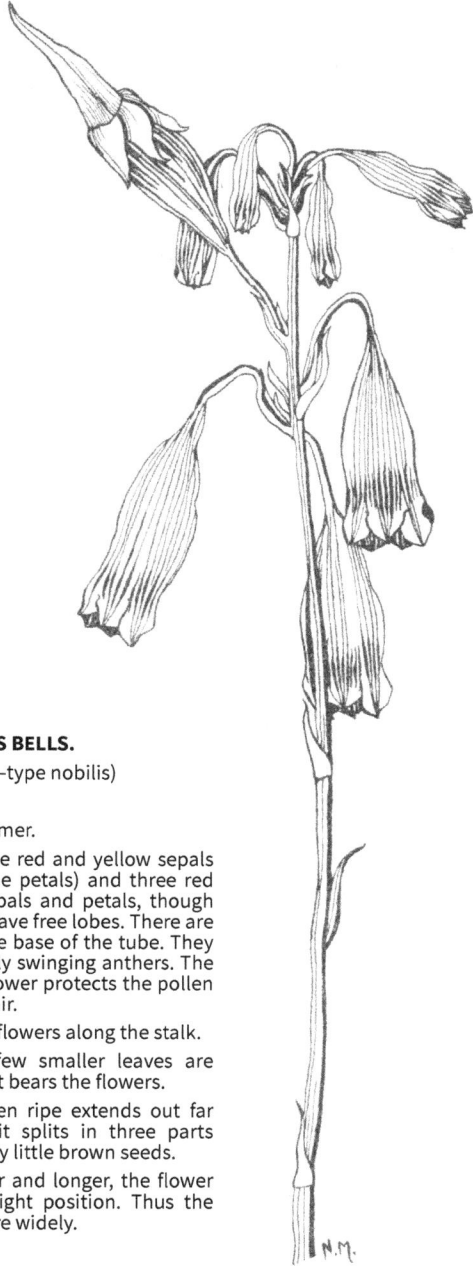

CHRISTMAS BELLS.

(BLANDFORDIA—type nobilis)

Family: Liliaceae.

Flowering season: summer.

Flowers: There are three red and yellow sepals (which look exactly like the petals) and three red and yellow petals. The sepals and petals, though joined together in a tube, have free lobes. There are six stamens attached to the base of the tube. They have long stalks and loosely swinging anthers. The drooping position of the flower protects the pollen from the dampness in the air.

There are usually many flowers along the stalk.

Leaves: Grass-like. A few smaller leaves are present along the stem that bears the flowers.

Fruit: A box which when ripe extends out far beyond the tube. When it splits in three parts lengthwise, it releases many little brown seeds.

As the fruit grows larger and longer, the flower gradually turns to an upright position. Thus the seeds can be scattered more widely.

N.M.

gradually turn their heads upward,and for the first time they look at the clear, blue sky, and watch the tiny wisps of white clouds drifting across it. That must be indeed a wonderful experience for them.

Of course, when the cases split open and the tiny, rough brown seeds are set free, great Sir Wind takes hold of them and whisks them away in all directions, then drops them down upon the ground and leaves them there to grow into more fine plants with the coming of next summer.

Right through the year I look forward to the coming of the Christmas Bells; and as soon as the very first one has unfolded its red and gold petals, I am there beside it, chattering with it and fluttering all around it (although it is always rather shy, and has very little to say in answer to my numerous questions).

The reason why I am able to pick it out immediately is that my favourite of all colours is red.

> Dainty, dancing Christmas Bells,
> 'Midst the swaying grasses,
> I can see you peeping out
> As the springtime passes—
> Passes from our bushy land
> To some other, distant strand,
> Leaving summer-tide to reign
> O'er the mountain and the plain.
>
> Dainty, dancing Christmas Bells,
> 'Midst the swaying grasses!

The Lord of the Orchid Gnomes

The Orchid Gnome

(CALOCHILUS—type grandiflorus)

> Little gnome,
> Here I roam
> Under bushes evermore
> Watching o'er my golden store.

The laws of the bushland and tradition are strange ones, you know. The other day two kookaburras were sitting on a branch of a huge gumtree right beside me. They were holding a sketchy kind of conversation on all manner of trifling things when one, glancing down at me, said to his friend: "Look! There goes the Lord of the Orchid Gnomes—I wonder where he keeps his gold!"

"Well, you'll never find out from him," replied the other. "You know what gnomes are like with their treasure, don't you?"

At this they both broke into peals of laughter, and flew away. But I began to wonder, and I went on wondering: I knew that fairy gnomes had gold, and I knew how carefully they guarded it, mostly around the roots of trees, or in thick, jungly forests—but I was an Orchid gnome, and had no gold at all—at least, not the kind you think of, in big shining nuggets. I have any amount of it in another way; and the funny thing about it is that nearly all plants in the world have it also, yet amongst the fairies, just because I am a gnome, I am the only one to get the credit for it.

Now, can you guess what that gold is? Why, it is the most beautiful of all—it is sunshine. And oh, how eager I am to capture those beams of light! Because, you see, as soon as I do, I have the magic power which only flowers possess of making the sweetest sugar with it, which I store away in my stems for when I may need it.

Perhaps you have never heard before how particular sunbeams are about what kind of thing they are captured by; for they are very lovable, industrious helpers to the earth, and so they refuse to be caught by anything which they feel is not going to use them thoroughly; and as it is only the green parts of any plant that can make sugar out of them, they take in the cooler red and blue colours of the rainbow and entrap them into making sugars out of water and the air around us, while they reflect back to us the hotter green portion which they cannot use so well. Aren't they cunning little things? You know, I wonder if you have ever thought of it, but every single green leaf which you see in your garden is really exactly the same as a little factory. So you just think how many factories you have all around you! And I don't suppose you thought you had one. Well, when my long, brown roots drink

GREAT BEARD ORCHID.

(CALOCHILUS—type grandiflorus)

Family: Orchidaceae.

Flowering seasons: Spring and early summer.

Flowers: Pale green and yellow in colour—sometimes quite a dark green. The labellum is large and covered with long purplish-red hairs. There are several blooms on the one stem.

Leaves: Long and narrow.

The plant is very graceful and sometimes 60cm high.

in little draughts of water from the earth and pass them along my stems until they finally enter my leaves, the tiny machines of all those factories begin to busy themselves, and the magic power which makes them able to work is the warmth of sunbeams.

And, try as people in your mortal world have done, to make sugar by themselves, they have really never succeeded, and always come back to us, asking us how we can possibly do it; but we hold that great secret forever within us. Now, if some cruel giant came along and swept every plant off the earth, what do you think would become of you, with no more bon-bons, or chocolates, or jellies? But, don't let us talk about it, shall we? It would be all too terrible, and there isn't any such giant after all.

And, by the way, I have a long, red beard, which is most attractive, and which I do hope you will take special notice of next time you meet me in the bushlands.

Gold, gold is the blazing sun,
For Orchid gnomes to hold—
Hold, hold in their leaves of green;
Gold are the sunbeams—gold!

"Each flower the dews have lightly wet,
And in the sky the stars are met,
And on the wave is deeper blue,
And on the leaf a browner hue,
And in the heaven that clear obscure,
So softly dark, and darkly pure,
Which follows the decline of day,
As twilight melts beneath the moon away."

—Byron

The Australian Bluebells

(WAHLENBERGIA—type gracilis)

There is a secret time of night when all the woods are magic—a beautiful time, lit by the twinkling stars, and otherwise wrapped in a cloak of deepest darkness. Mortals call it the "magic hour" and think it is always at midnight. And this is usually true, because, you see, the woods must be entirely free from humans before fairies can appear.

But in those **very** secret haunts, where mortal feet have never yet trodden upon the rich carpets of ferns and mosses, no sooner has the sunset faded and the twilight deepened than all the wildflowers come to life, as it were, and suddenly the bush is filled with tiny, fragile creatures who sail upon the wind and flutter to and fro like butterflies and soar high into the heavens and trip lightly as thistledown over the grass. They dance to the music of the gentle winds and in the soft brilliance of the stars, until a faint colouring in the east proclaims approaching day.

And it is to the chiming of my little bells of blue that the wildflowers listen. It is in answer to their call that they leave their trees or bushes and cast aside their frail disguise, becoming the sweetest and most beautiful of tiny beings that the world has ever seen.

Hush! Hush! For the sun has set,
The sun has set in the flaming west.
Hush! Hush! For the sounds of men
Have crept away to their welcome rest.

Wild winds, cease from your furious play,
And still your wrath for a little space,
For the woods are lonely and gone is the day,
And the nook you see is a fairy place!

Your boist'rous frolic for open hills
And frowning boulders and wastes was made,
But not for the magic of hidden rills
And the witching spell of a fairy glade.

Then come, ye fairies! I call you! List
To the tinkling sound of my bells of blue!
Oh, come, by the stars and moonbeams kissed,
To dance on the billows of falling dew!

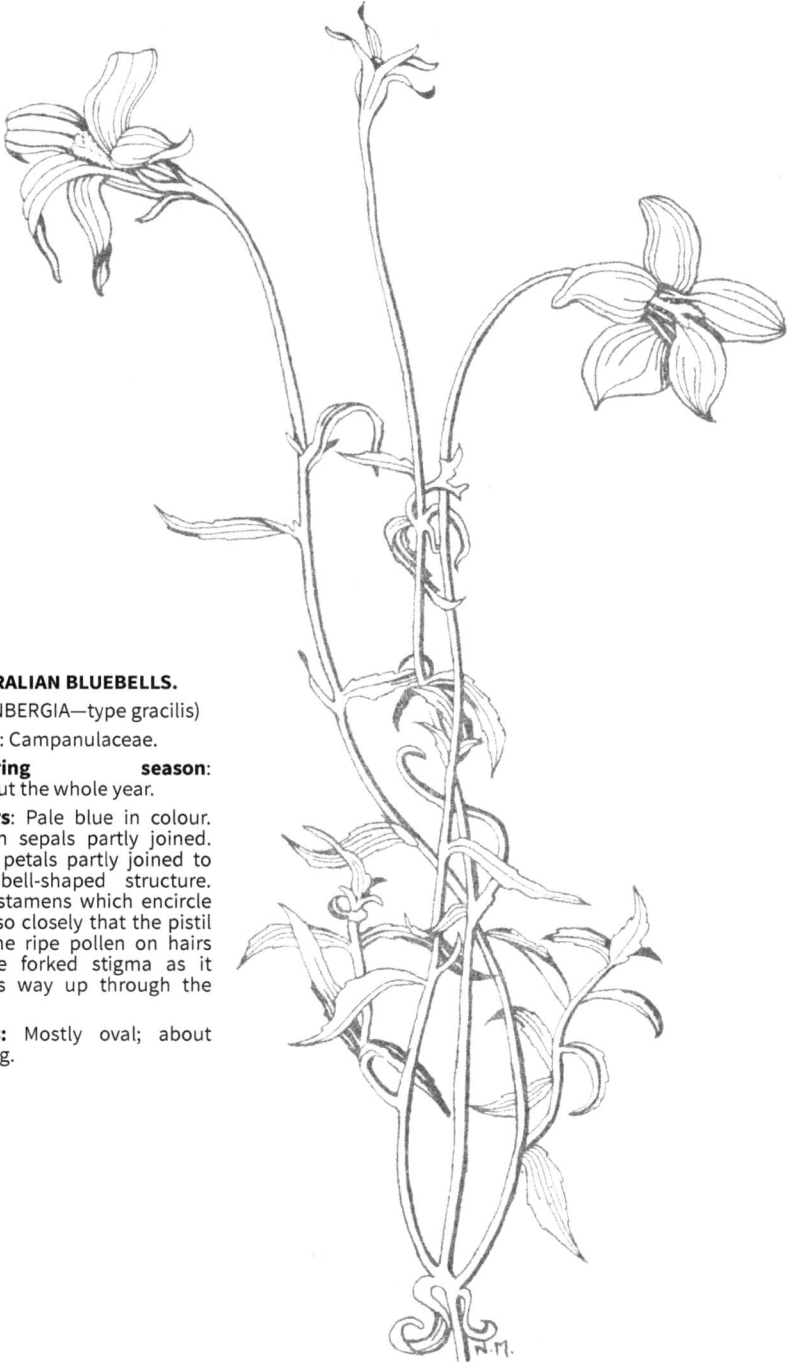

AUSTRALIAN BLUEBELLS.

(WAHLENBERGIA—type gracilis)

Family: Campanulaceae.

Flowering season: Throughout the whole year.

Flowers: Pale blue in colour. Five green sepals partly joined. Five blue petals partly joined to form a bell-shaped structure. Five free stamens which encircle the pistil so closely that the pistil gathers the ripe pollen on hairs below the forked stigma as it pushes its way up through the anthers.

Leaves: Mostly oval; about 25mm long.

The Lillipilly Fairy

(EUGENIA—type Smithii)

In spring and summertime the fairies are very happy, for in these seasons many more wildflowers come out than in any other —and fairies do love wildflowers.

Now I, the Lillipilly, also come out in tiny white blooms at these times, and you should just see the elves standing beside me clapping their hands with joy because they know that very soon my tree will be covered with big, round balls for them to play with.

My flowers grow together in large groups near the ends of branches; and it is a good thing they do, for if they did not, I am afraid no-one would notice them (as they are by no means big and handsome). Then, when the tiny sepals and petals and frail stamens shrivel away, the little balls begin to grow. Each one has a thin stem and when, after a short time, it decides to grow no more, it looks just like a beautiful cherry; but instead of being dark red in colour, it is pink and cream.

You can imagine, I am sure, how pretty my tree looks when it is covered with heavy bunches of purple, pink and cream balls, nestling in amongst the large, dark green leaves. Human children always seem to be ever so excited when they find me, at the side of a river or deep down in shady gullies. But the only thing they are sorry about is that almost as soon as they pick a branch of me laden with berries, the pretty balls begin to fall off one after the other until there are very few left.

"Oh," they sigh in disappointment, "the fairies did use bad gum when they were sticking these lillipillies on!" But they little know that the fairies are hovering all around them and can hear everything they say. Those tiny mischievous creatures with their gossamer frocks and sunshine wings laugh merrily to themselves, for it is they who, all unknown, are knocking off the berries as quickly as they can—because they know quite well that children have their own toys to play with and do not need the pretty soft, pink lillipillies with which the fairies love to play ball at the magic hour.

Oh, hide them, hide them behind those rocks,
Oh, pop them quickly in a deep, dark box—
Oh, hold them tightly and fly as fast
As elves and goblins when the night has passed!

And if you hide them where none can see,
And if you even as the lightning flee,
You'll still discover the elves have found
And knocked your berries to the soft, warm ground!

100

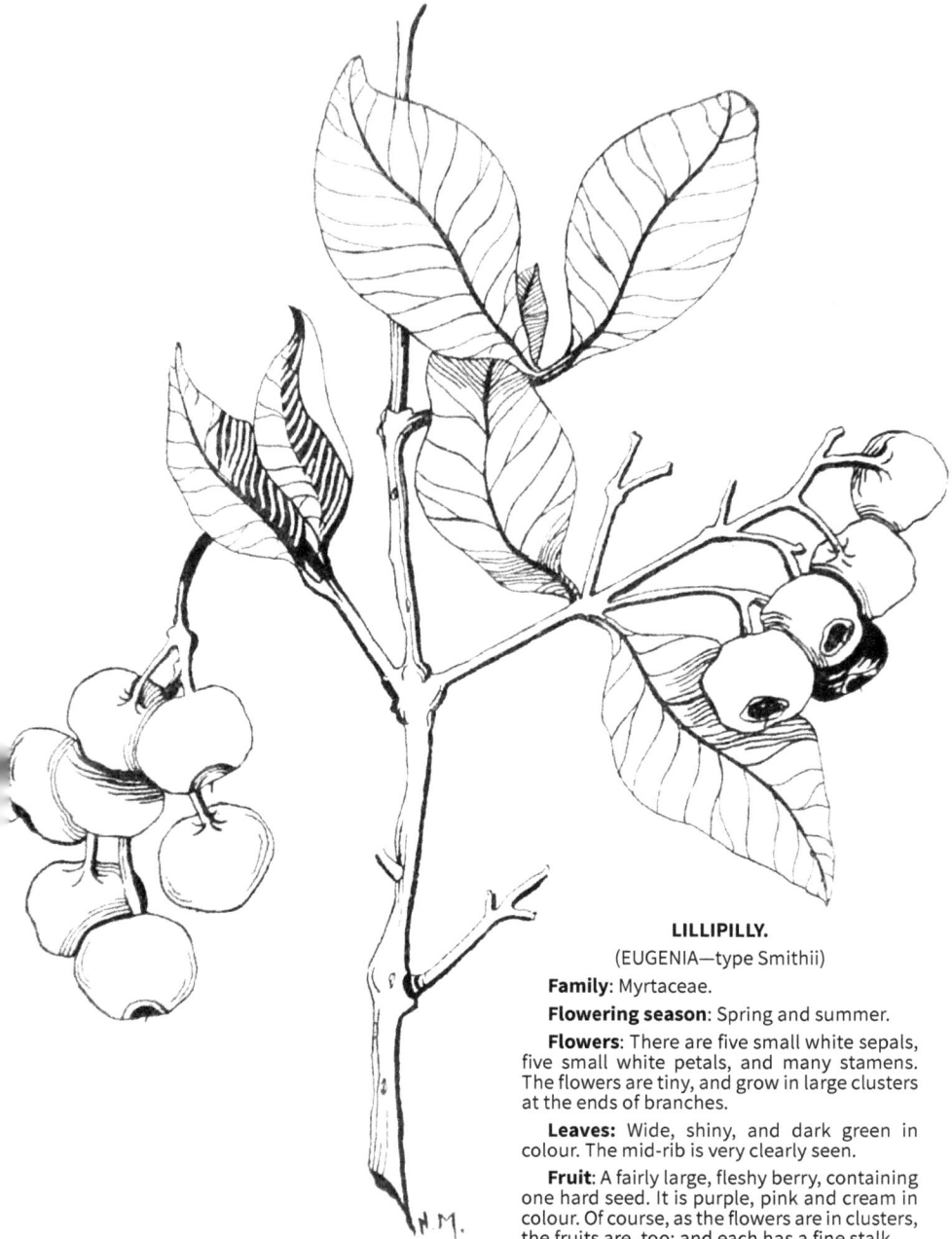

LILLIPILLY.

(EUGENIA—type Smithii)

Family: Myrtaceae.

Flowering season: Spring and summer.

Flowers: There are five small white sepals, five small white petals, and many stamens. The flowers are tiny, and grow in large clusters at the ends of branches.

Leaves: Wide, shiny, and dark green in colour. The mid-rib is very clearly seen.

Fruit: A fairly large, fleshy berry, containing one hard seed. It is purple, pink and cream in colour. Of course, as the flowers are in clusters, the fruits are, too; and each has a fine stalk.

101

The Growl of the Orchid Scrooge

(LYPERANTHUS—type nigricans)

Happy little child, pass by me,
And the songs of bell-birds follow;
Seldom do my flowers adorn me,
For my heart is full of sorrow.

And you will not find me dancing with the sunshine and shadows as do other wildflowers, for I much prefer sad loneliness; so I hardly ever come out in flowers at all, because I know that if I should, other fairies and elves, birds, mosquitoes and beetles would come and talk to me, bothering me with ceaseless conversation and playful tricks. All this nonsense I **cannot** bear, so, as I must put in some appearance upon the earth, I send up above the ground a funny, thick dwarf of a plant with a large, oval-shaped leaf—none of these flimsy-looking things; and I give it a respectable colour of as dark a green as Nature can possibly find for me.

In the meantime I stay well and truly underneath, where I cannot hear such exasperating gossip as, for instance:

"—Did you hear about Billie the bee yesterday, drinking so much honey out of Miss Waratah's honeypot that she was too drunk to see straight, and had to stumble upon a moss-bed near the Diamond Creek and stay there for over two hours?" or "— Did you know that Miss Isabelle Butterfly stayed out so late last night inquiring into the details of Mrs. Dragonfly's trip abroad to the other side of Crystal Lake that she couldn't find her way home and has been missing ever since?"

You can surely see how tired I must get with all this—what shall I call it? Underneath the ground is much quieter: I can sit there for months at a time, moping, without anyone interfering.

Sometimes, however, I do feel as if I would like to look at the day, so that makes me more miserable, as I cannot see day without coming into contact with the altogether rude and inconsiderate traffic of flying things. But if a bushfire has just passed over the place, leaving it black and lifeless, I smile to myself and pop my head out for a spell of a month or two. And then, if I don't get butterflies and birds and elves, I get humans—and they're worse. They talk and talk, and just because my flowers happen to be rather lovely to look at, with their dark red and purple tones and a little white, they have to pick me and fuss about with me and commit the atrocity of pressing me flat in a book. Of course, when this occurs I think it is time for a little interference on my part; so I turn coal-black all over—that teaches them not to meddle with me! I wonder if this is the only reason mortals have for calling me the "Undertaker."

Well, I am going now—good-bye!

RED BEAKS.

(LYPERANTHUS—type nigricans)

Family: Orchidaceae.

Flowering season: spring.

Flowers: Dark reddish-purple in colour. The sepals and petals are long and narrow. The "tongue" is white, with red veinings on the side-lobes. There are several flowers on the one stalk, but usually they do not appear unless a bushfire has swept over the place where the plants are growing. When dried, the flowers turn black.

Leaves: Large, oval in shape, and mottled.

The whole plant is usually only about 15cm high.

The Christmas Bush Fairy
(CERATOPETALUM—type gummiferum)

I suppose you have often heard it said that all nature is in harmony and Man alone is discord. Well, this is not entirely true, for there are wild animals in jungles that fight savagely, whilst in the plant kingdom there is a constant warfare which often results in the destruction or stunting of the smaller by the larger plants.

But I think it is true that men are the greatest destroyers of all, for no sooner have they made their appearance in some beautiful wooded country than the moss is trampled on, the ferns are trodden down and broken, the trees (before so grand and majestic) lie sadly on the ground; then after a time they are set upright once more, with all their leaves and branches broken away, as ugly telegraph poles. You see, we plants are so thoroughly defenceless when humans attack us.

Once upon a time, I thought I was safe, and that no-one would bother cutting me down—because I loved to imagine that I would be of no use to man. But very soon, I found that I had been mistaken; for I was by no means spared the sorrows of my companions. Mortals did not take long to discover that my reddish-coloured, soft wood could be made into tool handles, and many other things. So it was that we handsome trees began to fall, one after another, and at the present time you will seldom find us ten or twelve meters high—except in parts where humans have not bothered us. Mostly you see us only as very young bushes of an unambitious height. You will agree, I think, that such treatment is terribly discouraging.

So often have I heard people remark on my red "petals," that I think I had better make sure you never speak of them in that way, by telling you that they are not petals, but sepals. When my flowers first unfold they are tiny, white, and if it were not for the fact that many of them grow together, they would be hardly noticeable. The sepals are very small indeed, and the petals only a little larger. But as the fruits ripen, these sepals enlarge more and more until they are about 12mm long. At the same time, they change their colour, gradually becoming the loveliest red; and just about Christmas their colour is brightest. It is for this reason that I am called the Christmas Bush.

This is the height of my glory. All the year round I look forward to December, for I do enjoy looking beautiful and decorative—all plants do. Their flowers are their greatest pride.

CHRISTMAS BUSH.

(CERATOPETALUM—type gummiferum)

Family: Cunoniaceae.

Flowering seasons: Spring and early summer.

Flowers: When the flower first unfolds the five tiny sepals are white. There are five tiny white petals, and ten stamens. When the petals fall off and the fruit ripens, the sepals grow to a length of about 12mm, and at the same time change their white colour for one of beautiful red.

There are very many flowers, and they grow in clusters at the ends of branches.

Leaves: Each leaf is divided into three parts, which are called "leaflets." These are about 6cm long, and their edges are "toothed" (or saw-like).

The name "gummiferum" refers to the large amount of gum or "kino" that exudes from the cut bark.

Yet alas! Mortals cannot leave me alone even then, but must pick great armfuls of me to ornament their homes, leaving behind them in the bush only a few poor, forlorn little trees robbed of all their beauty.

I suppose I should be less selfish and not mind—but mortals also should be less selfish and not pick, don't you think?

Something else you may not know about me is that right inside my trunk there is a substance that looks like a gum from the plant's sap, but which is really what humans call a "kino" which is a dark red liquid formed mainly in between the bark and the central trunk. This is very pretty indeed, being red and transparent. Kino comes out when the bark is damaged and dries into a shiny, hard, red, and protective solid when the bark is damaged. Kino with its high tannin content is sometimes used as a medicinal treatment.

> Other blossoms lose their charm
> When their petals droop and die.
> Life for them is e'en as short
> As a zephyr's gentle sigh.
> Just a fleeting day or so
> Robs them of their vivid glow.
>
> Yet when all my petals fall,
> Beauty does not sadly fade.
> She, the sweetest fairy-soul—
> Sweetest soul that e'er was made—
> Turns my tree, with magic hand,
> To a crimson Fairyland.

"Thanks to the human heart by which we live,
Thanks to its tenderness, its joys, and fears,
To me the meanest flower that blows can give
Thoughts that do often lie too deep for tears."

—Wordsworth

Another Greenhood Fairy
(PTEROSTYLIS—type pedunculata)

Have you ever heard people say that you have to "train your eye" to the finding of certain things, like four-leafed clovers? Well, a short time ago, two humans were walking together along a bush-track at the side of which I was growing, when one, happening to notice me, said: "Look, there are some little Greenhoods! And there are two kinds of them also." Her friend, of course, looked where she had pointed and after a long while admitted that all she could see was a bit of fallen wood and much grass.

At this, the first speaker laughed heartily, and replied: "Well, they **are** there just the same. And before we return home tonight, you will be able to pick out Greenhoods as quickly as I can, because your eyes will have become accustomed to finding them." This sounded rather strange to me, but that night at the magic hour, I learned from my relations farther along the track that after a very little while, the second speaker did begin to find Greenhoods, and that she couldn't believe they had been as plentiful in the place where I was growing.

"And so," thought I to myself, "I and my fellow Greenhoods must be like four-leafed clovers in at least one respect."

Of course, I can understand why we are somewhat difficult to find. I suppose anything would be, which, growing amongst grasses, was itself green and brownish in colour.

Now, that first speaker whom I told you about must have been a quick observer indeed; for, if you remember, she noticed instantly not only that there were Greenhoods beside her, but also that there were two kinds. And if you look with sufficient care, little human, you will nearly always find that where I grow, that other kind grows, too. And if you happen to notice that other kind first, you are almost sure to meet me also very nearby. Because, you see, Pterostylis nutans and I are very fond of each other, and so we do not like to become separated any more than we possibly can. We are just sufficiently similar to form a link of likeness between us, and just sufficiently different to make us interesting to one another.

Firstly, we both have a spreading rosette of leaves at the base of our plant, and we are both fairly tall; and secondly, while Pterostylis nutans droops her head decidedly, I hold mine perfectly erect. This may not seem very important to humans, but it means a great deal to flowers. For, you understand, I can tell her all that is going on in the sky and when a storm is approaching, and she can tell me all that is going on along the ground and when an ant is approaching.

So that together, we gain quite an all-round knowledge of current events.

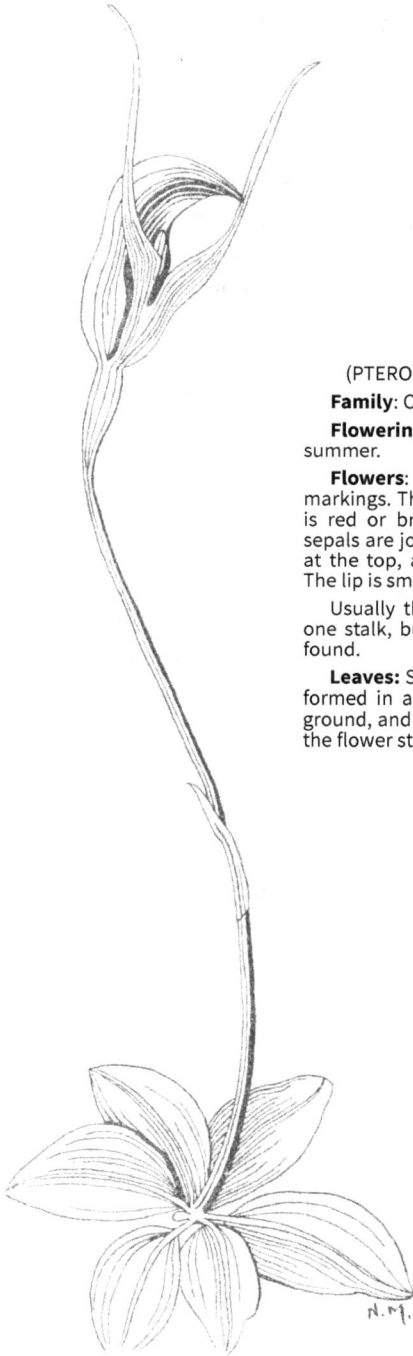

GREENHOOD.

(PTEROSTYLIS—type pedunculata)

Family: Orchidaceae.

Flowering seasons: Spring and early summer.

Flowers: Green in colour, with dark markings. The top of the flower particularly is red or brown in colour. The two front sepals are joined at the base but separated at the top, and are very long and narrow. The lip is small, and oval in shape.

Usually there is only one flower on the one stalk, but at times even three may be found.

Leaves: Sometimes fairly large. They are formed in a rosette which lies flat on the ground, and from the centre of which arises the flower stalk.

N.M.

109

The Needle Bush Fairy

(HAKEA—type acicularis)

Of course, I know why it is mortals call me the Needle Bush. It is because of my seemingly vicious leaves—long, narrow, and ending with a sharp point. They are just like rose thorns to **feel**, but to look at they are longer, finer and ever so much more numerous. Also, they are attached all over my stems, so that they stand out in every imaginable direction, and it is not possible for anyone to pick a tiny branch of me without getting badly pricked.

However, every part of me is not cruel, for in early springtime there are to be found amongst my unfriendly leaves the prettiest and gentlest little white or creamish flowers. While they are still in bud, they seem to be only a few stray, curly threads which have caught on to the branch by mistake. But as they unfold, you see that each "thread" is a separate flower, that there are quite a number of these blooms in each group, and that there are many groups all the way up the stem.

These flowers are very kind and mean no harm to anyone. But in reality my leaves are also kind—and I am sure you would agree with me if you knew them properly. You see, because my flowers are so frail and defenceless, they might easily come to much harm at the hands of rough bush creatures and mortals. But as it is, they live quite safely and happily because they know that while my leaves are around them, nothing can hurt them. So, every time you want to say how cruel those "needles" are, you must remember that they are only doing their very best to protect the little flowers you love so much to see. Also, you may notice that although they are more closely crowded together than mortals find convenient, they are quite far enough apart to allow the entrance of gentle insects (such as bees) who come to sip honey, have a little gossip and then carry away some pollen to another Needle Bush flower.

I wonder now if I have made you feel a wee bit more kindly towards my prickly leaves.

I do not for a moment doubt that you are already acquainted with my fruits, which have the queerest bumpy appearance, and end with a funny little point. They are thick and woody. Inside them there are two seeds, each with a pretty wing almost papery to feel. The wing, of course, makes it easy for the seed to fly about in the wind, and not reach the ground too soon, before it has had time to enjoy a few adventures and the fresh, open air.

You will look for me next time you come to the bush, won't you? And I do hope you will make friends with my leaves. They are really lonely little beings because no one ever seems to like them, so they will appreciate your thoughtfulness very much.

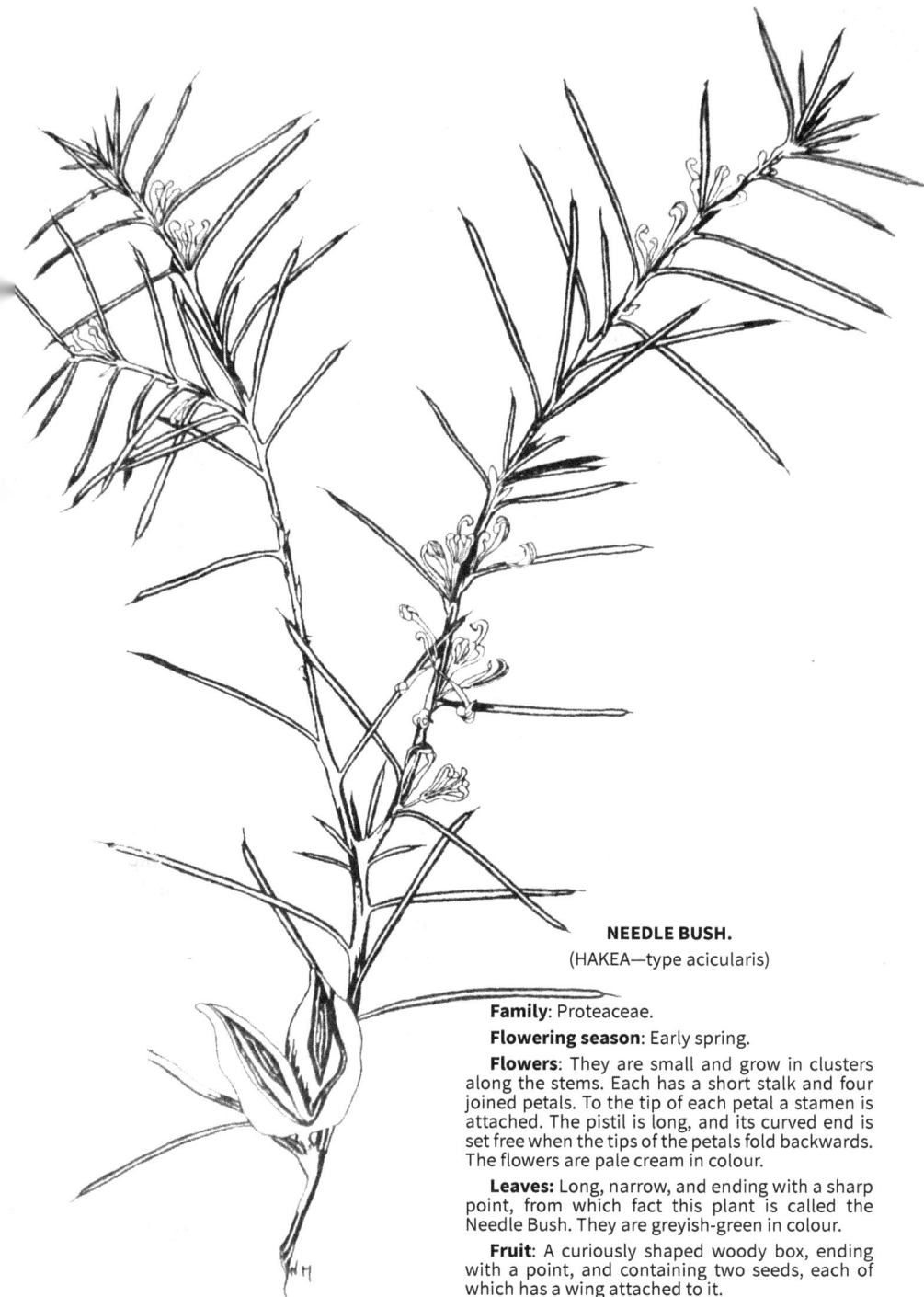

NEEDLE BUSH.

(HAKEA—type acicularis)

Family: Proteaceae.

Flowering season: Early spring.

Flowers: They are small and grow in clusters along the stems. Each has a short stalk and four joined petals. To the tip of each petal a stamen is attached. The pistil is long, and its curved end is set free when the tips of the petals fold backwards. The flowers are pale cream in colour.

Leaves: Long, narrow, and ending with a sharp point, from which fact this plant is called the Needle Bush. They are greyish-green in colour.

Fruit: A curiously shaped woody box, ending with a point, and containing two seeds, each of which has a wing attached to it.

111

The Rock Lily or Orchid King

(DENDROBIUM—type speciosum)

Do you know when the little silver moonbeams dance from the very top of the sky, along the milky way, through the still, silent trees to the ground, and there play with tiny dewdrops and fluffy-winged moths? Well, it is only at these times that I can easily become a fairy, for I love the moon as other Orchids do the sun, and others, the wind. Of course, I could not live without the good old sun to give me strength and warmth—yet, well, I don't know how it is, but I often think that millions of years ago my frail petals were woven with threads of moonlight as they wandered to the Earth.

I can remember a long time back when all the bush orchids gathered together in a great assembly and, with one voice, proclaimed me their king; and what do you think? So that even humans would realise my all-powerful position they gave my most important petal any amount of purple spots, as we had heard that such a colour to humans was a sign of royalty. And to this very day I still wear them because I think they look so becoming on their creamy background.

And now I must tell you something rather funny which amused me quite a lot. One afternoon in the middle of last September I was giving a garden party to a few of my subjects, amongst whom were little Miss Pink Fingers, or in other words, Lady Caladenia carnea, Lord Calochilus grandiflorus, Countess Dipodium punctatum, and Sir Cryptostylis subulata or, the Knight of the Fairy Garter, as he is usually known.

Just as we were about to ask the earth for a little more water to drink, we heard human voices approaching, so we kept as still and quiet as could be, because we hoped no one would notice us, as mortals always seem to want to pick us and then drop us by the wayside without any thought at all.

Soon, however, a little girl with long, fair hair came running down the bush track, and, her searching eyes having picked us out immediately, she called:

"Oh, Mother, just look at these pretty flowers!" Then she came right up to me and, taking hold of my big, thick stem, she said:

"And look, Mother, here is a Rock Lily!"

We all felt like shrieking with laughter, but of course that would have been terrible.

"Well, don't pick it, dear," said a kind-faced lady, just now making her appearance, "You know, that is one of the protected flowers; and don't pick any of the others, either, for they are all Orchids and also protected."

With this the little girl let me go, and saying: "But aren't they pretty,

ROCK LILY or the ORCHID KING.

(DENDROBIUM—type speciosum)

Family: Orchidaceae.

Flowering season: spring.

Flowers: Creamish-coloured. The lip ("labellum") is beautified with purple spots. Usually the flowers are much crowded together, very numerous and fragrant.

Leaves: Shiny, stiff and leathery. Their mid-rib is very clearly seen.

Stems: Thick, and deeply grooved. It is in the stems that a great deal of the plant's food is stored.

The plant does not grow in the soil, mostly. It is found growing to perfection on trees and rocks. However it does not steal any food from the trees upon which it rests; therefore it is not a parasite.

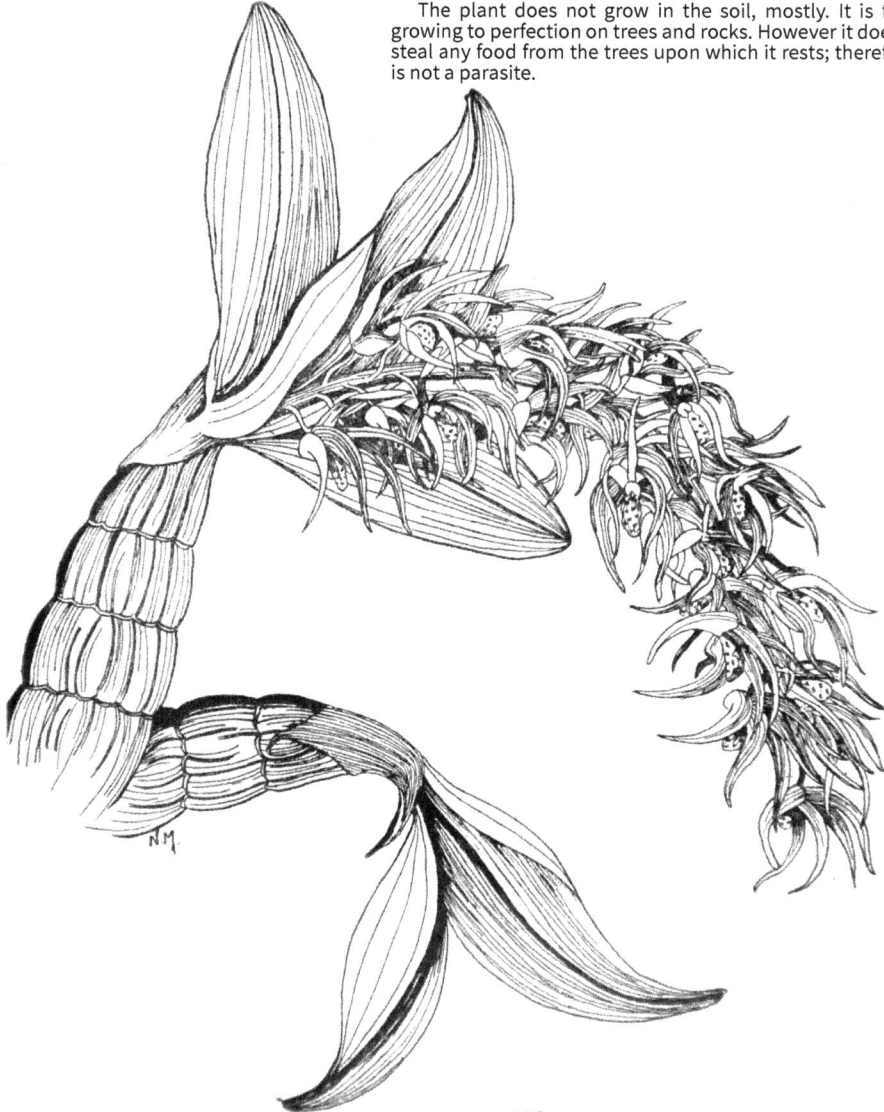

113

Mother, all those pink and white and red and yellow flowers?" she continued her journey along the track.

As soon as they had gone there was a great deal of tittering and giggling and whispering amongst my guests. Little Miss Pink Fingers leaned over to the Knight of the Fairy Garter and whispered something in his ear, to which they both screwed up their eyes and giggled. Lord Calochilus took the Countess's arm and spoke rather seriously, then turning to me, said: "Most mighty sovereign, is it any wonder that humans call you a 'lily,' and a 'rock' one at that, when you keep your stem so ungainly and thick and hard? Is it any wonder that they will not even give you the credit of being an Orchid? Look, for an instance, at the slender daintiness of Miss Pink Fingers, and my friend the Countess!"

At this, both the pretty ladies looked clown to the very tips of their toes and blushed a little pinker than usual.

By this time I thought it would befit me to say something for myself, so I spread out a sheaf of creamy blossoms and said:

"Ah! you little seem to realise that I am your king, and that as such, my position is not a dainty one, but a serious and responsible one: I have to teach you an admiration of determination. It is for this reason that I live on hard, dry rocks, on the faces of cliffs and on the bark of trees—yet I wouldn't think of being a parasite and stealing from them who have such a lot to do to nourish their own tremendous heights and widths."

And so I went on explaining to my now very serious listeners how, because I became hungry the same as they did and needed food, my stems, leaves and roots had to get busy and do all they could to help me. "It is when the rain falls," I continued, "that my opportunity comes. Then my stems, leaves and roots absorb just as many of the raindrops as they can, and store them away in hundreds of little compartments so that in times of drought I shall have plenty of nourishment to go on with. And you well know, because you have them too, those tiny compartments in our stems where we keep the sweetest and finest sugar, which mortals cannot even see without using strong 'glass eyes' as well as their own.

My gallant Knight now stepped forward and knelt before me saying, "Indeed we have a wonderful king in Orchid land, and we are all very proud of you: apart from your beautiful ideals you also have flowers whose whose delicate colour and perfume are admired by every one of your little subjects!"

So that is the story of my garden party in the middle of last September, and of how I let my Orchid guests into a few of my guarded secrets.

I was giving a garden party.

The Tea-tree Fairy

(LEPTOSPERMUM—type flavescens)

Amongst mortals, it is the custom, I have heard, for people to become friends and to seek each other's company when there is a bond of sympathy or affection between them. In the bush world, this is also the case sometimes; although it usually happens that different birds and insects become most friendly with the flowers from which they can easiest sip honey. So it is that Ms. Bee shuns long, narrow, tube-like flowers because these mostly store their honey at the very bottom of their tube, and her tongue is not nearly long enough to reach it. Mr. Honeysucker, on the other hand, is on the best of terms with such flowers, because his beak is long enough.

I wonder if humans always make friends the way I have been told they do, or if they also are over-interested sometimes in how much honey they can get from their fellow humans.

Well, if you look carefully at my cream-coloured flowers, you will see that the five outspread petals are arranged round a sort of shallow little cup which holds the honey. This is **so** shallow, and the sweet liquid it contains is so easily found, that you will at once guess what insect it is who is my special friend—Ms. Bee.

She is the principal one; but, of course, there are many others. In fact, any insect at all with a short tongue and a fondness for honey is likely to visit me quite often. So I am never lonely.

And now, if you look again at the floor of my cup, you will notice that it is divided into five parts; and that as the petals and stamens around it fall away, it becomes the top of my fruit. This fruit enlarges, growing harder and more woody all the time, until finally (when the narrow seeds inside it are ripe, and when the season is dry) it splits open along the now five deep grooves, and the seeds are set free.

I am sure you will not have difficulty in finding me, as I grow in all the eastern parts of Australia. I am a tall shrub and have rather small, oblong leaves which, though green, have a lot of yellow in them too. And of course, you will easily be able to recognise my cream-coloured flowers.

TEA-TREE.

(LEPTOSPERMUM—type
flavescens)

Family: Myrtaceae.

Flowering seasons: Spring and summer.

Flowers: They have five green sepals, the bases of which are joined to form a round tube. The five petals are outspread and cream-coloured. There are many stamens arranged around a shallow cup, from the centre of which a short pistil grows, and which contains honey. The flowers do not grow in clusters, but singly.

Leaves: About 25mm long, oblong in shape, and yellowish-green in colour. They grow fairly close together.

Fruit: Cup-shaped. When the seeds are ripe and the season is dry, the fruit splits open across the top in five places, and many small seeds fall out.

The plant is a tall shrub.

117

The Romance of the Little White Dove

(CALADENIA—type praecox)

Have you ever wished from the very bottom of your heart to see a fairy? Have you ever crept on tip-toe from the softly curling fronds of your fernery to a large chrysanthemum or a shy blue violet, and peered right in to see if you could catch one by surprise, and not finding one at all, ask a little tearfully: "Oh, dear Miss Violet, haven't you seen a fairy pass this way to-day?" And that timid flower which was, perhaps, a fairy just pretending all the time, winked at you—and a tiny spark of mischief flashed into the heart of the flower.

Well, while you look so unsuccessfully for fairies, maybe you have heard birds singing way up in the trees. They are really laughing at you, because they can see them everywhere: perched on your hand, ruffling up your hair—you thought it was a breeze that **blew** your hair didn't you? No! It was about half a dozen elves **swinging** on it!

Birds can see and hear fairies easier than any other material creature. And for this reason it was that ever so many years ago, when the world was young and beautiful, I, a little white dove, with a pale pink colour under my wings, used to carry messages from flowers to fairies and from fairies to flowers. I always remember a tiny Microtis Orchid once conveying a message by me to Fairyland: "Please send a squadron of goblins to Grassland Grove—a snail is approaching." Another time, a little spring fairy whispered in my ear: "Hurry down to where the Orchid gnomes are growing, and tell their leader to get all his followers out in flowers during today. At midnight I shall visit them and paint their long beards a brilliant red. They will like that news." Always in these rapid flights of mine I used to think what lovely little beings bushland Orchids were, and right inside me I wished that I could be one too; but I never said a word about it in Fairyland.

One time, though, I was wandering around the bush, talking to this Orchid and that one, and wishing more than ever that I could be one of them when all of a sudden I heard a tiny, very frightened, silvery cry. I flew to where it came from and alas! There, terribly caught and entangled in a great spider web, was the beautiful fairy queen. It was all the work of the Giant of Spiders before he was defeated by the Knight of the Fairy Garter.

I said a few words of comfort and promise to her and then, as fast as my wings could carry me, I flew to where the grand army of dwarfs and goblins was resting, waiting to be called upon, and told them what had happened.

WHITE DOVES.

(CALADENIA—type praecox)

Family: Orchidaceae.

Flowering season: Winter and early spring.

Flowers: White in colour, with pink or green markings. The "tongue" is fringed, and is marked with purple in the centre. Usually there are two or three flowers on the one stem.

This Orchid is to be found only in Victoria, and seldom grows taller than 15 cm.

In less than two seconds the whole army had landed at the entrance to the spider web, and charged right into it. This occupied the Giant while the fairy king unbound his lovely queen, and together they all flew back to Fairyland. Later I heard that the Giant spent two whole days rebuilding his web, it was so huge and strong.

But can you guess what happened? The next evening, when the stars were trooping up in hundreds and thousands to their positions in the sky, the queen sent for me to go to her court, and when I arrived she said that because I had saved her life she would grant me anything my heart desired. I thanked her ever and ever so much, and of course, told her that more than anything in the world I would like to be a little wild Orchid. She smiled, and kissed my head so gently that I shall never forget my joy that night, or her loveliness.

According to her order I was escorted to the mortal world by a whole troop of fairies, as well as by the king and queen themselves. And after much celebration, dancing, singing and laughter, the queen touched me softly with the tip of her wand; and, looking at myself in a tiny brook nearby, I saw the loveliest white flower just streaked with the tiniest bit of pale pink. But the magic wand had touched me so lightly that some of the downy feathers on my head had not quite disappeared, and to this very day they still remain to adorn my smallest petal!

"In all places, then, and in all seasons,
    Flowers expand their light and soul-like wings,
Teaching us, by most persuasive reasons,
    How akin they are to human things."

—Longfellow

The Bottlebrush Fairy

(CALLISTEMON—type lanceolatus)

My name Callistemon comes from two Greek words, one meaning "beauty," the other "stamen." So that the whole name means "beautiful stamen"; and if you remember having seen me in any of your bushwalks, you will realise how it is people call me that.

The anthers of my stamens are rather small and yellow, but the long, fine stalks (or "filaments") are bright red in colour. Each flower has a great many stamens, and as there are any amount of flowers crowded closely together near the tip of the stem, you can understand how pretty and attractive I seem to those who meet me.

I am glad my stamens are so numerous and beautiful, because the rest of my flower is such that no one would ever bother to look at it more than once. My fate would indeed be a sad one if I did not possess those stamens. Why! Not even the Honeysuckers would go to the trouble of visiting and talking to me and, of course, carrying away my pollen to another Bottlebrush somewhere else in Bushland. My five little petals are a brown-yellowy-green colour, and my five sepals are small and green.

Usually, we red Bottlebrush shrubs do not grow separately (that would be lonesome indeed) but many of us together. So that in spring and summer, when we come out in flower, we certainly do add a bright splash of colour to our surroundings. I remember once how a little girl, walking through the bush with her mother and father, came across us and, clasping her hands in admiration, said: "Mother dear, see how the woodlands are blushing!"

If you look at my smooth, oblong leaves, you will see all over them tiny round dots. These, as my friend Boronia has explained to you, are glands filled with oil. However, although we are similar in this, I do not belong to her family, but to that which humans call Myrtaceae. I am proud of this fact, because Myrtaceae is a most distinguished family, having as some of its members the Eucalyptus, the Lillipilly and Teatrees. If your very near relation were a Gum tree or a Lillipilly, wouldn't you feel ever so proud too?

I suppose you have all noticed my little fruits, have you? Of course, as my flowers are crowded together, my fruits are too; and they just look like a whole family of fairy-cups. Now, when the right season comes (that is, when the weather is nice and dry) they all split open at the top and a host of tiny seeds falls out. These are blown away by the wind to their new

BOTTLEBRUSH.

(CALLISTEMON—type
lanceolatus)

Family: Myrtaceae.

Flowering seasons: Spring and summer.

Flowers: There are five small green sepals and five red or dirty green petals. The stamens are very numerous, long, and crimson in colour. Their anthers are yellow. The pistil is also crimson and long.

The flowers are crowded together very closely around the stem, and have no stalks. As red is the favourite colour of Honeysuckers, it is likely that these birds visit the flowers often.

Leaves: They are oblong, and usually about five centimeters long. All over them, tiny oil dots can be seen.

Fruits: Round and woody. They only split open in dry weather, when they release many small seeds.

123

homes—sometimes far away from and sometimes near to the plant from which they came. This is a great adventure for the little seeds, and I can assure you they look forward to it ever so much.

Now, before I say good-bye, I must point out to you something which occurs with all Bottlebrushes. You would think it strange if the stems of roses continued to grow through the tops of the blooms, wouldn't you? And yet, when you see a crowded group of Bottlebrush flowers, you are almost sure to notice growing on above it a leafy shoot, which is really the continuation of the stem. So it is that on a single branch you will often find, first a collection of little fruits; then, above these, a group of flowers; and above these again, the youngest part of the stem growing on and on, which will soon be adorned with another collection of flowers.

This is funny, don't you think? But Bottlebrushes are not the only plants that do it. Next time you go for a bush walk, you could enjoy yourself very much searching for more. And if you were to look at Teatrees (Leptospermums) very carefully, I am sure you would not be disappointed.

Oh the whip-bird's call and the bracken sea,
The green, immortal minstrelsy,
 The tow'ring trees, the mystic glen
 So far from the abodes of men—
A sky-roofed sanctuary of moss and ferns,
Where man the harmonies of Nature learns.

What though a thousand duties to me float
As blatant voices on a city-note?
 Their cruel enslavement I must fly,
 Or in their strangling meshes die!
Here are the curling fronds, the fragrant earth, the flowers,
What else does man require to fill his fleeting hours?

TheHeath-Leaved Banksia Fairy

(BANKSIA—type ericifolia)

When I look at the Boronias, Wattles, Teatrees, Flannel Flowers and many others of my bush companions, I begin to realise that there is nothing frail or dainty about me at all. Of course, if it happened that every one of us was dainty, there would be little variation indeed, and humans would soon complain about the monotony of Bushland. So I suppose I should be grateful that at least I can help to make things interesting.

But, despite the thick appearance of my large groups of flowers, I have never heard anyone condemn me as being ugly. On the contrary, everyone seems to praise me for my handsomeness and my flame-like colouring. Sometimes I am only deep yellow, but other times I have, mixed with the yellow, such a brilliant reddish colour, that children imagine me to be a scrap of bushfire capturedmagic and fastened to my tall, woody shrub.

I wonder if you have ever taken one of those thick, uptight stalks of mine covered with blooms, and counted the number of flowers on it. If you have, no doubt you have been surprised to find that there are several hundreds— each separate flower being so small, yet so perfect. Sometimes I feel that Nature takes a special delight in tiny things, making them so absolutely faultless that the most powerful microscope can only reveal more marvels in them. I wonder how many things made by humans could be tested in the same way and prove themselves as perfect.

Well, all those little flowers are attached to the thick stem (or "axis") in pairs. And if you were to start at the bottom of the stalk and with your pencil follow round and round it from one pair to the next, you would see that you were gradually approaching the top; and when you had finished you would find that you had traced out the form of a spiral. So you would say that the flowers were "spirally arranged."

Now, after the flowers come the fruits—and with these I know you are all well acquainted, for they are the famous "Banksia men." They certainly do look fearsome, as a whole lot of woody nuts are buried in a dark mass of what seems to be brown, wiry hair, but which is in reality all that remains of the vividly-coloured flowers.

Each nut holds inside it two seeds which have wings, and it is so anxious about their welfare that it simply refuses to open out and let them escape

HEATH-LEAVED BANKSIA.
(BANKSIA—type ericifolia)
Family: Proteaceae.
Flowering seasons: All through the year.

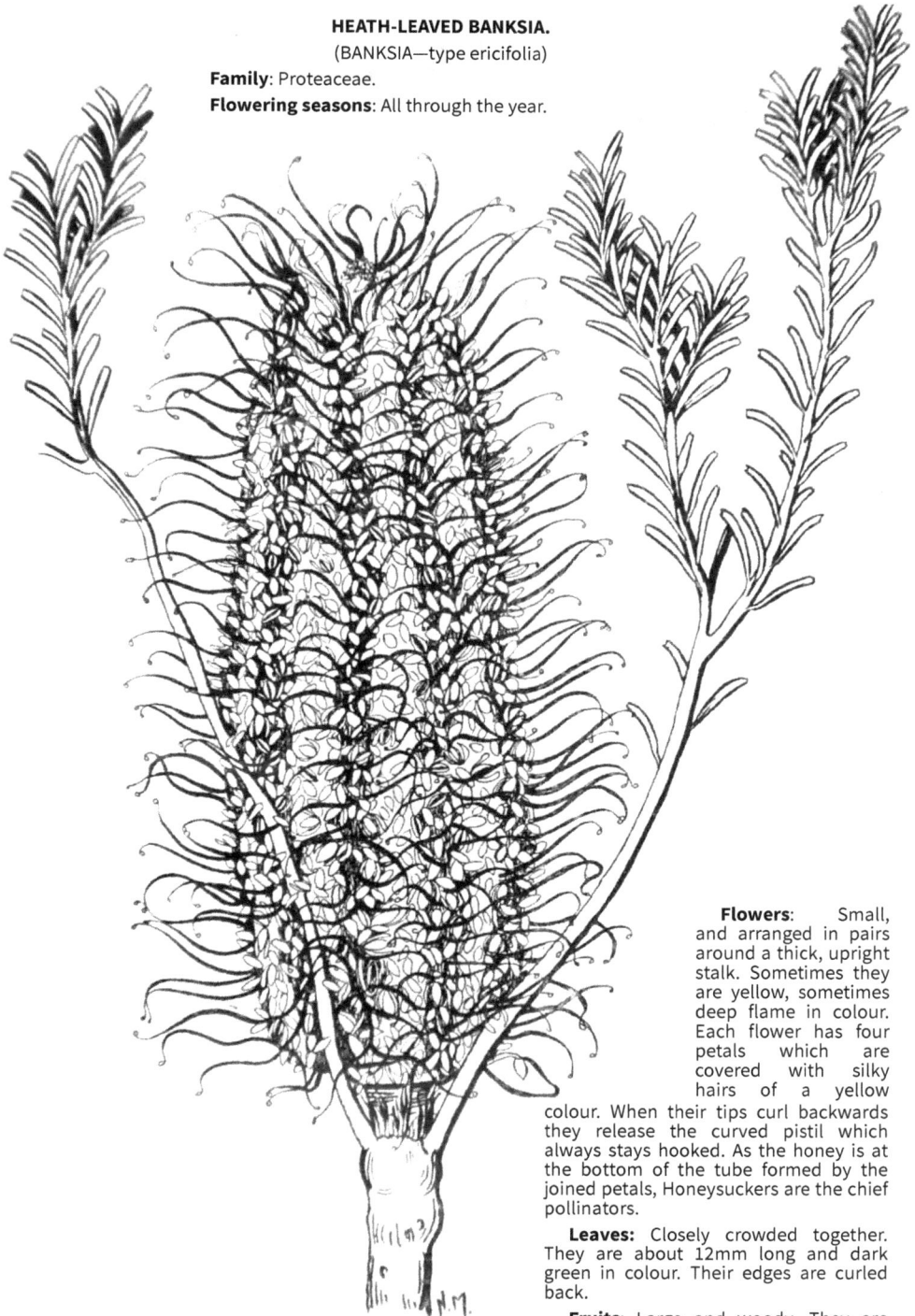

Flowers: Small, and arranged in pairs around a thick, upright stalk. Sometimes they are yellow, sometimes deep flame in colour. Each flower has four petals which are covered with silky hairs of a yellow colour. When their tips curl backwards they release the curved pistil which always stays hooked. As the honey is at the bottom of the tube formed by the joined petals, Honeysuckers are the chief pollinators.

Leaves: Closely crowded together. They are about 12mm long and dark green in colour. Their edges are curled back.

Fruits: Large and woody. They are embedded in the remains of the flowers, which become brown and wiry.

127

into the bush world until a sufficiently dry season arrives. It is because of this that some nuts wait as long as several years before attempting to open.

It is true, I know, that Banksia men used to do dreadful things once upon a time, carrying off poor little fairies and gumnuts and making them captive. But a short time ago, while they were asleep, a few brave fairies came right up to them and brought them a terrible dream which made them feel all the things being done to them that they themselves had done to the little bush folk. And let me tell you a secret: even since that dream, they have been remarkably well-behaved, and at the present time they are even succeeding in making themselves loved amongst the fairies and elves.

Pterostylis Baptistii is always looking down upon me.

The Humble Fairy
(MICROTIS—type porrifolia)

Although I am one of the most humble of Orchids, and hardly ever am I paid any attention by humans, you will find me really very lovely when you look at me closely, for I have such a delicate green colour, mixed with a little white and yellow, and though you may think I am too small to have all the complicated parts in me that my lordlier relations possess, I really have. So just you think what a true masterpiece of Nature I am, when men have to use powerful microscopes (as they call them) to see me properly, yet I am so perfect and complete; and my "labellum" wears the prettiest little scalloped-edged frock, which only a flower-fairy of my size could possibly wear.

I think it must be a definite characteristic of ours to form very strong family affections which make it most difficult for us to part, so you will always see about twenty or more of us on the one stem.

And to make it even better, wherever we decide to settle down we form a real little colony, inhabited by simply dozens of our plants.

This is also very useful because by ourselves we are so small that our friends, the mosquitoes, would not be much impressed with us, and Pterostylis longifolia has explained to you how necessary we find them in our lives.

As it is, however, we look quite beautiful to them, though hardly at all to humans, for at the first glance we are so similar to all the grass in the midst of which we grow. Then, what should we do alone if an enemy should appear? Our tiny forms, you see, make us really quite defenceless, so that it takes a large army of us to be equal to a caterpillar or a snail.

Would you believe it that Pterostylis Baptistii is always looking down upon me, and spreading out her leafy rosette to show me how grand she looks—just because I only happen to have one leaf which is long and narrow? It makes me feel a little peevish at the time, I will admit, but I know it shouldn't, as such behaviour only occurs when we are flowers—when our little material bodies are all we can see; yet at the magic hour when we become fairies— when we become the flower-souls, we cannot help being kind and loving to everyone. We often think human souls must be like that also, but we hardly ever see them to really know.

I should simply love you to come out to the bush and talk to me a little when you have time. I am not very particular about where I live, so you may

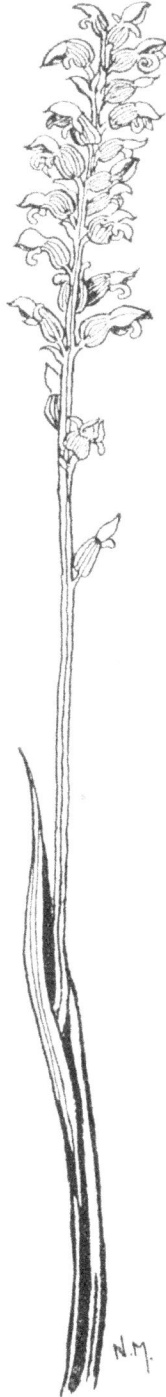

MICROTIS—type porrifolia

Family: Orchidaceae.

Flowering season: spring.

Flowers: Green in colour. They are very minute and numerous. The two side sepals are curved backward and the middle one is hooded. The column has two tiny ear-like wings.

The flowers are crowded closely together.

Leaves: Long, smooth and narrow.

Sometimes the plant is extremely small, but other times it may attain a height of one metre. It grows on barren grasslands as well as in swampy regions.

131

come across me almost anywhere from dry, barren hilltops to grassy flats, river banks and quite swampy places.

But I am a real little spring flower! In fact I love spring so much that I always get excited when I know she is approaching. Consequently I come out in bloom in good time to see her make her triumphal entry into the Australian bush.

And now, my small mortal friend, the magic hour is over.

Once more we must arrange ourselves up and down swaying stems and become speechless flowers before we are seen by the eyes of day. Slowly, slowly, I see all my fairy companions drifting away, so, from all the shy bush-flowers who have spoken to you tonight, I say

"GOOD-BYE"

Good-Bye

The shades of night where fairies dwell
Are floating now beyond the trees
And ferns and flowers, across whose eyes
There sweeps a quiv'ring breeze.

And little swaying stems that stood
All unadorned through night's deep hours,
Are holding now, as Dawn awakes,
Some timid bushland flowers!

The witchery of shadows and
The magic spell of dreams have fled;
The bush was filled with fairies—now,
'Tis filled with flowers instead!

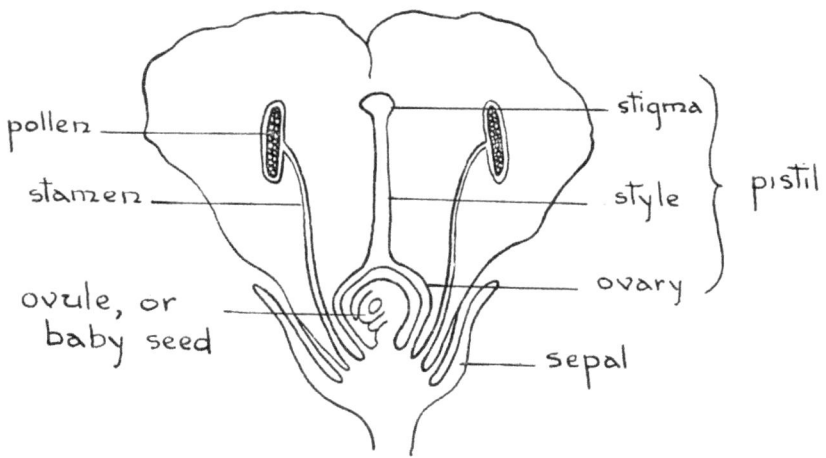

pollen

stamen

ovule, or
baby seed

stigma

style

ovary

sepal

pistil

www.ingramcontent.com/pod-product-compliance
Lightning Source LLC
Chambersburg PA
CBHW071944260326
41914CB00004B/760